Police and Criminal Evidence Act 1984 (PACE)

CODE D

Revised

CODE OF PRACTICE FOR THE IDENTIFICATION OF PERSONS BY POLICE OFFICERS

February 2017

Commencement - Transitional Arrangements

This code has effect in relation to any identification procedure carried out after 00:00 on 23 February 2017.

GRAN*GIS* UK Publishing

Adapted and Published by GRANGIS (Grand Register Library).
Online: www.grangis.com.
E-mail: contact@grangis.com.

In this version:
ISBN: 979-8-88559-092-1

Note: Title, sub-title and version of this publication is as described. For the most recent information please visit www.gov.uk.

About this publication:

enquiries www.gov.uk/contactus
download www.gov.uk/government/publications

Contents

1 Introduction

1.1 This Code of Practice concerns the principal methods used by police to identify people in connection with the investigation of offences and the keeping of accurate and reliable criminal records. The powers and procedures in this code must be used fairly, responsibly, with respect for the people to whom they apply and without unlawful discrimination. Under the Equality Act 2010, section 149 (Public sector Equality Duty), police forces must, in carrying out their functions, have due regard to the need to eliminate unlawful discrimination, harassment, victimisation and any other conduct which is prohibited by that Act, to advance equality of opportunity between people who share a relevant protected characteristic and people who do not share it, and to foster good relations between those persons. The Equality Act also makes it unlawful for police officers to discriminate against, harass or victimise any person on the grounds of the 'protected characteristics' of age, disability, gender reassignment, race, religion or belief, sex and sexual orientation, marriage and civil partnership, pregnancy and maternity when using their powers. See *Note 1A.*

1.2 In this Code, identification by an eye-witness arises when a witness who has seen the offender committing the crime and is given an opportunity to identify a person suspected of involvement in the offence in a video identification, identification parade or similar procedure. These eye-witness identification procedures which are in Part A of section 3 below, are designed to:

- test the eye-witness' ability to identify the suspect as the person they saw on a previous occasion
- provide safeguards against mistaken identification.

While this Code concentrates on visual identification procedures, it does not prevent the police making use of aural identification procedures such as a "voice identification parade", where they judge that appropriate. See *Note 1B.*

1.2A In this Code, separate provisions in Part B of section 3 below, apply when any person, including a police officer, is asked if they recognise anyone they see in an image as being someone who is known to them and to test their claim that they recognise that person. These separate provisions are not subject to the eye-witnesses identification procedures described in *paragraph 1.2.*

1.2B Part C applies when a film, photograph or image relating to the offence or any description of the suspect is broadcast or published in any national or local media or on any social networking site or on any local or national police communication systems.

1.3 Identification by fingerprints applies when a person's fingerprints are taken to:

- compare with fingerprints found at the scene of a crime
- check and prove convictions
- help to ascertain a person's identity.

1.3A Identification using footwear impressions applies when a person's footwear impressions are taken to compare with impressions found at the scene of a crime.

1.4 Identification by body samples and impressions includes taking samples such as a cheek swab, hair or blood to generate a DNA profile for comparison with material obtained from the scene of a crime, or a victim.

1.5 Taking photographs of arrested people applies to recording and checking identity and locating and tracing persons who:

- are wanted for offences
- fail to answer their bail.

1.6 Another method of identification involves searching and examining detained suspects to find, e.g., marks such as tattoos or scars which may help establish their identity or whether they have been involved in committing an offence.

1.7 The provisions of the Police and Criminal Evidence Act 1984 (PACE) and this Code are designed to make sure fingerprints, samples, impressions and photographs are taken, used and retained, and identification procedures carried out, only when justified and necessary for preventing, detecting or investigating crime. If these provisions are not observed, the application of the relevant procedures in particular cases may be open to question.

1.8 The provisions of this Code do not authorise, or otherwise permit, fingerprints or samples to be taken from a person detained solely for the purposes of assessment under section 136 of the Mental Health Act 1983.

Note for Guidance

1A In paragraph 1.1, under the Equality Act 1949, section 149, the 'relevant protected characteristics' are: age, disability, gender reassignment, pregnancy and maternity, race, religion/belief, sex and sexual orientation. For further detailed guidance and advice on the Equality Act, see: https://www.gov.uk/guidance/equality-act-2010-guidance.

1B See Home Office Circular 57/2003 *"Advice on the use of voice identification parades".*

2 General

2.1 This Code must be readily available at all police stations for consultation by:

- police officers and police staff
- detained persons
- members of the public

2.2 The provisions of this Code:

- include the *Annexes*
- do not include the *Notes for guidance.*

2.3 Code C, paragraph 1.4 and the *Notes for guidance* applicable to those provisions apply to this Code with regard to a suspected person who may be mentally disordered or otherwise mentally vulnerable.

2.4 Code C, paragraphs 1.5 and 1.5A and the *Notes for guidance* applicable to those provisions apply to this Code with regard to a suspected person who appears to be under the age of 18.

2.5 Code C, paragraph 1.6 applies to this Code with regard to a suspected person who appears to be blind, seriously visually impaired, deaf, unable to read or speak or has difficulty communicating orally because of a speech impediment.

2.6 In this Code:

- 'appropriate adult' means the same as in Code C, *paragraph 1.7*
- 'solicitor' means the same as in Code C, *paragraph 6.12*

and the *Notes for guidance* applicable to those provisions apply to this Code.

- where a search or other procedure under this Code may only be carried out or observed by a person of the same sex as the person to whom the search or procedure applies, the gender of the detainee and other persons present should be established and recorded in line with Annex L of Code C.

2.7 References to a custody officer include any police officer who, for the time being, is performing the functions of a custody officer, see *paragraph 1.9* of Code C.

2.8 When a record of any action requiring the authority of an officer of a specified rank is made under this Code, subject to *paragraph 2.18,* the officer's name and rank must be recorded.

2.9 When this Code requires the prior authority or agreement of an officer of at least inspector or superintendent rank, that authority may be given by a sergeant or chief inspector who has been authorised to perform the functions of the higher rank under PACE, section 107.

2.10 Subject to *paragraph 2.18*, all records must be timed and signed by the maker.

2.11 Records must be made in the custody record, unless otherwise specified. In any provision of this Code which allows or requires police officers or police staff to make a record in their report book, the reference to 'report book' shall include any official report book or electronic recording device issued to them that enables the record in question to be made and dealt with in accordance with that provision. References in this Code to written records, forms and signatures include electronic records and forms and electronic confirmation that identifies the person completing the record or form.

Chief officers must be satisfied as to the integrity and security of the devices, records and forms to which this *paragraph* applies and that use of those devices, records and forms satisfies relevant data protection legislation.

(taken from *Code C paragraph 1.17)*.

2.12 If any procedure in this Code requires a person's consent, the consent of a:

- mentally disordered or otherwise mentally vulnerable person is only valid if given in the presence of the appropriate adult
- juvenile is only valid if their parent's or guardian's consent is also obtained unless the juvenile is under 14, when their parent's or guardian's consent is sufficient in its own right. If the only obstacle to an identification procedure in *section 3* is that a juvenile's parent or guardian refuses consent or reasonable efforts to obtain it have failed, the identification officer may apply the provisions of *paragraph 3.21* (suspect known but not available). See *Note 2A*.

2.13 If a person is blind, seriously visually impaired or unable to read, the custody officer or identification officer shall make sure their solicitor, relative, appropriate adult or some other person likely to take an interest in them and not involved in the investigation is available to help check any documentation. When this Code requires written consent or signing, the person assisting may be asked to sign instead, if the detainee prefers. This paragraph does not require an appropriate adult to be called solely to assist in checking and signing documentation for a person who is not a juvenile, or mentally disordered or otherwise mentally vulnerable (see *Note 2B* and Code C *paragraph 3.15*).

2.14 If any procedure in this Code requires information to be given to or sought from a suspect, it must be given or sought in the appropriate adult's presence if the suspect is mentally disordered, otherwise mentally vulnerable or a juvenile. If the appropriate adult is not present when the information is first given or sought, the procedure must be repeated in the presence of the appropriate adult when they arrive. If the suspect appears deaf or there is doubt about their hearing or speaking ability or ability to understand English, the custody officer or identification officer must ensure that the necessary arrangements in accordance with Code C are made for an interpreter to assist the suspect.

2.15 Any procedure in this Code involving the participation of a suspect who is mentally disordered, otherwise mentally vulnerable or a juvenile must take place in the presence of the appropriate adult. See Code C *paragraph 1.4*.

2.15A Any procedure in this Code involving the participation of a witness who is or appears to be mentally disordered, otherwise mentally vulnerable or a juvenile should take place in the presence of a pre-trial support person unless the witness states that they do not want a support person to be present. A support person must not be allowed to prompt any identification of a suspect by a witness. See *Note 2AB*.

2.16 References to:

- 'taking a photograph', include the use of any process to produce a single, still or moving, visual image
- 'photographing a person', should be construed accordingly
- 'photographs', 'films', 'negatives' and 'copies' include relevant visual images recorded, stored, or reproduced through any medium
- 'destruction' includes the deletion of computer data relating to such images or making access to that data impossible

2.17 This Code does not affect or apply to, the powers and procedures:

(i) for requiring and taking samples of breath, blood and urine in relation to driving offences, etc, when under the influence of drink, drugs or excess alcohol under the:

- Road Traffic Act 1988, sections 4 to 11
- Road Traffic Offenders Act 1988, sections 15 and 16
- Transport and Works Act 1992, sections 26 to 38;

(ii) under the Immigration Act 1971, Schedule 2, paragraph 18, for taking photographs, measuring and identifying and taking biometric information (not including DNA) from persons detained or liable to be detained under that Act, Schedule 2, paragraph 16 (Administrative Provisions as to Control on Entry etc.); or for taking fingerprints in accordance with the Immigration and Asylum Act 1999, sections 141 and 142(4), or other methods for collecting information about a person's external physical characteristics provided for by regulations made under that Act, section 144;

(iii) under the Terrorism Act 2000, Schedule 8, for taking photographs, fingerprints, skin impressions, body samples or impressions from people:

- arrested under that Act, section 41,
- detained for the purposes of examination under that Act, Schedule 7, and to whom the Code of Practice issued under that Act, Schedule 14, paragraph 6, applies ('the terrorism provisions')

(iv) for taking photographs, fingerprints, skin impressions, body samples or impressions from people who have been:

- arrested on warrants issued in Scotland, by officers exercising powers mentioned in Part X of the Criminal Justice and Public Order Act 1994;
- arrested or detained without warrant by officers from a police force in Scotland exercising their powers of arrest or detention mentioned in Part X of the Criminal Justice and Public Order Act 1994.

Note: In these cases, police powers and duties and the person's rights and entitlements whilst at a police station in England and Wales are the same as if the person had been arrested in Scotland by a Scottish police officer.

2.18 Nothing in this Code requires the identity of officers or police staff to be recorded or disclosed:

(a) in the case of enquiries linked to the investigation of terrorism;

(b) if the officers or police staff reasonably believe recording or disclosing their names might put them in danger.

In these cases, they shall use their warrant or other identification numbers and the name of their police station. *See Note 2D.*

2.19 In this Code:

(a) 'designated person' means a person other than a police officer, who has specified powers and duties conferred or imposed on them by designation under section 38 or 39 of the Police Reform Act 2002;

(b) any reference to a police officer includes a designated person acting in the exercise or performance of the powers and duties conferred or imposed on them by their designation.

2.20 If a power conferred on a designated person:

(a) allows reasonable force to be used when exercised by a police officer, a designated person exercising that power has the same entitlement to use force;

(b) includes power to use force to enter any premises, that power is not exercisable by that designated person except:

(i) in the company, and under the supervision, of a police officer; or

(ii) for the purpose of:

- saving life or limb; or
- preventing serious damage to property.

2.21 In the case of a detained person, nothing in this Code prevents the custody officer, or other police officer or designated person given custody of the detainee by the custody officer for the purposes of the investigation of an offence for which the person is detained, from allowing another person (see *(a)* and *(b)* below) to carry out individual procedures or tasks at the police station if the law allows. However, the officer or designated person given custody remains responsible for making sure the procedures and tasks are carried out correctly in accordance with the Codes of Practice. The other person who is allowed to carry out the procedures or tasks must be *someone who at that time* is:

(a) under the direction and control of the chief officer of the force responsible for the police station in question; or;

(b) providing services under contractual arrangements (but without being employed by the chief officer the police force), to assist a police force in relation to the discharge of its chief officer's functions.

2.22 Designated persons and others mentioned in *sub-paragraphs (a)* and *(b)* of *paragraph 2.21* must have regard to any relevant provisions of the Codes of Practice.

Notes for guidance

2A For the purposes of paragraph 2.12, the consent required from a parent or guardian may, for a juvenile in the care of a local authority or voluntary organisation, be given by that authority or organisation. In the case of a juvenile, nothing in paragraph 2.12 requires the parent, guardian or representative of a local authority or voluntary organisation to be present to give their consent, unless they are acting as the appropriate adult under paragraphs 2.14 or 2.15. However, it is important that a parent or guardian not present is fully informed before being asked to consent. They must be given the same information about the procedure and the juvenile's suspected involvement in the offence as the juvenile and appropriate adult. The parent or guardian must also be allowed to speak to the juvenile and the appropriate adult if they wish. Provided the consent is fully informed and is not withdrawn, it may be obtained at any time before the procedure takes place.

2AB The Youth Justice and Criminal Evidence Act 1999 guidance "Achieving Best Evidence in Criminal Proceedings" indicates that a pre-trial support person should accompany a vulnerable witness during any identification procedure unless the witness states that they do not want a support person to be present. It states that this support person should not be (or not be likely to be) a witness in the investigation.

2B *People who are seriously visually impaired or unable to read may be unwilling to sign police documents. The alternative, i.e. their representative signing on their behalf, seeks to protect the interests of both police and suspects.*

2C *Not used*

2D *The purpose of paragraph 2.18(b) is to protect those involved in serious organised crime investigations or arrests of particularly violent suspects when there is reliable information that those arrested or their associates may threaten or cause harm to the officers. In cases of doubt, an officer of inspector rank or above should be consulted.*

3 Identification and recognition of suspects

Part (A) Identification of a suspect by an eye-witness

3.0 This part applies when an eye-witness has seen a person committing a crime or in any other circumstances which tend to prove or disprove the involvement of the person they saw in a crime, for example, close to the scene of the crime, immediately before or immediately after it was committed. It sets out the procedures to be used to test the ability of that eye-witness to identify a person suspected of involvement in the offence ('the suspect') as the person they saw on the previous occasion. This part does not apply to the procedure described in Part B (see Note 3AA) which is used to test the ability of someone who is not an eye-witness, to recognise anyone whose image they see.

3.1 A record shall be made of the description of the suspect as first given by the eye-witness . This record must:

(a) be made and kept in a form which enables details of that description to be accurately produced from it, in a visible and legible form, which can be given to the suspect or the suspect's solicitor in accordance with this Code; and

(b) unless otherwise specified, be made before the eye-witness takes part in any identification procedures under *paragraphs 3.5 to 3.10, 3.21, 3.23* or Annex E (Showing Photographs to Eye-Witnesses).

A copy of the record shall where practicable, be given to the suspect or their solicitor before any procedures under *paragraphs 3.5* to *3.10, 3.21 or 3.23* are carried out. See *Note 3E.*

3.1A References in this Part:

(a) to the identity of the suspect being 'known' mean that there is sufficient information known to the police to establish, in accordance with Code G (Arrest), that there are reasonable grounds to suspect a particular person of involvement in the offence;

(b) to the suspect being 'available' mean that the suspect is immediately available, or will be available within a reasonably short time, in order that they can be invited to take part in at least one of the eye-witness identification procedures under *paragraphs 3.5* to *3.10* and it is practicable to arrange an effective procedure under *paragraphs 3.5 to 3.10*; and

(c) to the eye-witness identification procedures under *paragraphs 3.5* to *3.10* mean:

- Video identification (*paragraphs 3.5* and *3.6*);
- Identification parade (*paragraphs 3.7* and *3.8*); and
- Group identification (*paragraphs 3.9* and *3.10*).

(a) Cases when the suspect's identity is not known

3.2 In cases when the suspect's identity is not known, an eye-witness may be taken to a particular neighbourhood or place to see whether they can identify the person they saw on a previous occasion. Although the number, age, sex, race, general description and style of clothing of other people present at the location and the way in which any identification is made cannot be controlled, the principles applicable to the formal procedures under *paragraphs 3.5* to *3.10* shall be followed as far as practicable. For example:

(a) where it is practicable to do so, a record should be made of the eye-witness' description of the person they saw on the previous occasion, as in *paragraph 3.1(a)*, before asking the eye-witness to make an identification;

(b) Care must be taken not provide the eye-witness with any information concerning the description of the suspect (if such information is available) and not to direct the eye-witness' attention to any individual unless, taking into account all the circumstances, this cannot be avoided. However, this does not prevent an eye-witness being asked to look carefully at the people around at the time or to look towards a group or in a particular direction, if this appears necessary to make sure that the witness does not overlook a possible suspect simply because the eye-witness is looking in the opposite direction and also to enable the eye-witness to make comparisons between any suspect and others who are in the area;

(c) where there is more than one eye-witness, every effort should be made to keep them separate and eye-witnesses should be taken to see whether they can identify a person independently;

(d) once there is sufficient information to establish, in accordance with *paragraph 3.1A(a)*, that the suspect is 'known', e.g. after the eye-witness makes an identification, the provisions set out from *paragraph 3.4* onwards shall apply for that and any other eye-witnesses in relation to that individual;

(e) the officer or police staff accompanying the eye-witness must record, in their report book, the action taken as soon as practicable and in as much detail, as possible. The record should include:

   (i) the date, time and place of the relevant occasion when the eye-witness claims to have previously seen the person committing the offence in question or in any other circumstances which tend to prove or disprove the involvement of the person they saw in a crime (see *paragraph 3.0*); and

   (ii) where any identification was made:

   - how it was made and the conditions at the time (e.g., the distance the eye-witness was from the suspect, the weather and light);
   - if the eye-witness's attention was drawn to the suspect; the reason for this; and
   - anything said by the eye-witness or the suspect about the identification or the conduct of the procedure.

See *Note 3F*

3.3 An eye-witness must not be shown photographs, computerised or artist's composite likenesses or similar likenesses or pictures (including 'E-fit' images) if in accordance with *paragraph 3.1A*, the identity of the suspect is known and they are available to take part in one of the procedures under *paragraphs 3.5* to *3.10*. If the suspect's identity is not known, the showing of any such images to an eye-witness to see if they can identify a person whose image they are shown as the person they saw on a previous occasion must be done in accordance with *Annex E*.

(b) Cases when the suspect is known and available

3.4 If the suspect's identity is known to the police (see *paragraph 3.1A(a)*) and they are available (see *paragraph 3.1A(b)*), the identification procedures that may be used are set out in *paragraphs 3.5* to *3.10* below as follows:

   (i) video identification;

   (ii) identification parade; or

   (iii) group identification.

(i) Video identification

3.5 A 'video identification' is when the eye-witness is shown images of a known suspect, together with similar images of others who resemble the suspect. *Moving* images must be used unless the conditions in sub-paragraph (a) or (b) below apply:

(a) this sub-paragraph applies if:

   (i) the identification officer, in consultation with the officer in charge of the investigation, is satisfied that because of aging, or other physical changes or differences, the appearance of the suspect has significantly changed since the previous occasion when the eye-witness claims to have seen the suspect (see *paragraph 3.0* and *Note 3ZA*);

(ii) an image (moving or still) is available which the identification officer and the officer in charge of the investigation reasonably believe shows the appearance of the suspect as it was at the time the suspect was seen by the eye-witness; and

(iii) having regard to the extent of change and the purpose of eye-witness identification procedures (see *paragraph 3.0*), the identification officer believes that that such an image should be shown to the eye-witness.

In such a case, the identification officer may arrange a video identification procedure using the image described in (ii). In accordance with the 'Notice to suspect' (see *paragraph 3.17(vi)),* the suspect must first be given an opportunity to provide their own image(s) for use in the procedure but it is for the identification officer and officer in charge of the investigation to decide whether, following (ii) and (iii), any image(s) provided by the suspect should be used.

A video identification using an image described above may, at the discretion of the identification officer be arranged in addition to, or as an alternative to, a video identification using *moving* images taken after the suspect has been given the information and notice described in *paragraphs 3.17* and *3.18*.

See *paragraph 3.21* and *Note 3D* in any case where the suspect deliberately takes steps to frustrate the eye-witness identification arrangements and procedures.

(b) this sub-paragraph applies if, in accordance with *paragraph 2A* of *Annex A* of this Code, the identification officer does not consider that replication of a physical feature or concealment of the location of the feature can be achieved using a moving image. In these cases, still images may be used.

3.6 Video identifications must be carried out in accordance with *Annex A*.

(ii) Identification parade

3.7 An 'identification parade' is when the eye-witness sees the suspect in a line of others who resemble the suspect.

3.8 Identification parades must be carried out in accordance with *Annex B*.

(iii) Group identification

3.9 A 'group identification' is when the eye-witness sees the suspect in an informal group of people.

3.10 Group identifications must be carried out in accordance with *Annex C*.

Arranging eye-witness identification procedures – duties of identification officer

3.11 Except as provided for in *paragraph 3.19*, the arrangements for, and conduct of, the eye-witness identification procedures in *paragraphs 3.5* to *3.10* and circumstances in which any such identification procedure must be held shall be the responsibility of an officer not below inspector rank who is not involved with the investigation ('the identification officer'). The identification officer may direct another officer or police staff, see *paragraph 2.21*, to make arrangements for, and to conduct, any of these identification procedures and except as provided for in *paragraph 7* of *Annex A,* any reference in this section to the identification officer includes the officer or police staff to whom the arrangements for, and/or conduct of, any of these procedure has been delegated. In delegating these arrangements and procedures, the identification officer must be able to supervise effectively and either intervene or be contacted for advice. Where any action referred to in this paragraph is taken by another officer or police staff at the direction of the identification officer, the outcome shall, as soon as practicable, be reported to the identification officer. For the purpose of these procedures, the identification officer retains overall responsibility for ensuring that the procedure complies with this Code and in addition, in the case of detained suspect, their care and treatment until returned to the custody officer. Except as permitted by this Code, no officer or any other person involved with the investigation of the case against the suspect may take any part in these procedures or act as the identification officer.

This paragraph does not prevent the identification officer from consulting the officer in charge of the investigation to determine which procedure to use. When an identification procedure is required, in the interest of fairness to suspects and eye-witnesses, it must be held as soon as practicable.

Circumstances in which an eye-witness identification procedure must be held

3.12 If, before any identification procedure set out in *paragraphs 3.5* to *3.10* has been held

(a) an eye-witness has identified a suspect or purported to have identified them; or

(b) there is an eye-witness available who expresses an ability to identify the suspect; or

(c) there is a reasonable chance of an eye-witness being able to identify the suspect,

and the eye-witness in (a) to (c) has not been given an opportunity to identify the suspect in any of the procedures set out in *paragraphs 3.5* to *3.10*, then an identification procedure shall be held if the suspect disputes being the person the eye-witness claims to have seen on a previous occasion (see *paragraph 3.0*), unless:

(i) it is not practicable to hold any such procedure; or

(ii) any such procedure would serve no useful purpose in proving or disproving whether the suspect was involved in committing the offence, for example

- where the suspect admits being at the scene of the crime and gives an account of what took place and the eye-witness does not see anything which contradicts that; or
- when it is not disputed that the suspect is already known to the eye-witness who claims to have recognised them when seeing them commit the crime.

3.13 An eye-witness identification procedure may also be held if the officer in charge of the investigation, after consultation with the identification officer, considers it would be useful.

Selecting an eye-witness identification procedure

3.14 If, because of *paragraph 3.12*, an identification procedure is to be held, the suspect shall initially be invited to take part in a video identification unless:

(a) a video identification is not practicable; or

(b) an identification parade is both practicable and more suitable than a video identification; or

(c) *paragraph 3.16* applies.

The identification officer and the officer in charge of the investigation shall consult each other to determine which option is to be offered. An identification parade may not be practicable because of factors relating to the witnesses, such as their number, state of health, availability and travelling requirements. A video identification would normally be more suitable if it could be arranged and completed sooner than an identification parade. Before an option is offered the suspect must also be reminded of their entitlement to have free legal advice, see Code C, *paragraph 6.5*.

3.15 A suspect who refuses the identification procedure in which the suspect is first invited to take part shall be asked to state their reason for refusing and may get advice from their solicitor and/or if present, their appropriate adult. The suspect, solicitor and/or appropriate adult shall be allowed to make representations about why another procedure should be used. A record should be made of the reasons for refusal and any representations made. After considering any reasons given, and representations made, the identification officer shall, if appropriate, arrange for the suspect to be invited to take part in an alternative which the officer considers suitable and practicable. If the officer decides it is not suitable and practicable to invite the suspect to take part in an alternative identification procedure, the reasons for that decision shall be recorded.

3.16 A suspect may initially be invited to take part in a group identification if the officer in charge of the investigation considers it is more suitable than a video identification or an identification parade and the identification officer considers it practicable to arrange.

Notice to suspect

3.17 Unless *paragraph 3.20* applies, before any eye-witness identification procedure set out in *paragraphs 3.5* to *3.10* is arranged, the following shall be explained to the suspect:

(i) the purpose of the procedure (see *paragraph 3.0*);

(ii) their entitlement to free legal advice; see Code C, *paragraph 6.5*;

(iii) the procedures for holding it, including their right, subject to *Annex A, paragraph 9*, to have a solicitor or friend present;

(iv) that they do not have to consent to or co-operate in the procedure;

(v) that if they do not consent to, and co-operate in, a procedure, their refusal may be given in evidence in any subsequent trial and police may proceed covertly without their consent or make other arrangements to test whether an eye-witness can identify them, see *paragraph 3.21;*

(vi) whether, for the purposes of a video identification procedure, images of them have previously been obtained either:

- in accordance with *paragraph 3.20*, and if so, that they may co-operate in providing further, suitable images to be used instead; or
- in accordance with *paragraph 3.5(a)*, and if so, that they may provide their own images for the identification officer to consider using.

(vii) if appropriate, the special arrangements for juveniles;

(viii) if appropriate, the special arrangements for mentally disordered or otherwise mentally vulnerable people;

(ix) that if they significantly alter their appearance between being offered an identification procedure and any attempt to hold an identification procedure, this may be given in evidence if the case comes to trial, and the identification officer may then consider other forms of identification, see *paragraph 3.21* and *Note 3C*;

(x) that a moving image or photograph may be taken of them when they attend for any identification procedure;

(xi) whether, before their identity became known, the eye-witness was shown photographs, a computerised or artist's composite likeness or similar likeness or image by the police, see *Note 3B;*

(xii) that if they change their appearance before an identification parade, it may not be practicable to arrange one on the day or subsequently and, because of the appearance change, the identification officer may consider alternative methods of identification, see *Note 3C*;

(xiii) that they or their solicitor will be provided with details of the description of the suspect as first given by any eye-witnesses who are to attend the procedure or confrontation, see *paragraph 3.1*.

3.18 This information must also be recorded in a written notice handed to the suspect. The suspect must be given a reasonable opportunity to read the notice, after which, they should be asked to sign a copy of the notice to indicate if they are willing to co-operate with the making of a video or take part in the identification parade or group identification. The signed copy shall be retained by the identification officer.

3.19 In the case of a detained suspect, the duties under *paragraphs 3.17* and *3.18* may be performed by the custody officer or by another officer or police staff not involved in the investigation as directed by the custody officer, if:

(a) it is proposed to release the suspect in order that an identification procedure can be arranged and carried out and an inspector is not available to act as the identification officer, see *paragraph 3.11*, before the suspect leaves the station; or

(b) it is proposed to keep the suspect in police detention whilst the procedure is arranged and carried out and waiting for an inspector to act as the identification officer, see *paragraph 3.11,* would cause unreasonable delay to the investigation.

The officer concerned shall inform the identification officer of the action taken and give them the signed copy of the notice. See *Note 3C.*

3.20 If the identification officer and officer in charge of the investigation suspect, on reasonable grounds that if the suspect was given the information and notice as in *paragraphs 3.17* and *3.18*, they would then take steps to avoid being seen by a witness in any identification procedure, the identification officer may arrange for images of the suspect suitable for use in a video identification procedure to be obtained before giving the information and notice. If suspect's images are obtained in these circumstances, the suspect may, for the purposes of a video identification procedure, co-operate in providing new images which if suitable, would be used instead, see *paragraph 3.17(vi).*

(c) Cases when the suspect is known but not available

3.21 When a known suspect is not available or has ceased to be available, see *paragraph 3.1A*, the identification officer may make arrangements for a video identification (see paragraph 3.5 and Annex A). If necessary, the identification officer may follow the video identification procedures using any suitable moving or still images and these may be obtained covertly if necessary. Alternatively, the identification officer may make arrangements for a group identification without the suspect's consent (see Annex C *paragraph 34*). See *Note 3D.* These provisions may also be applied to juveniles where the consent of their parent or guardian is either refused or reasonable efforts to obtain that consent have failed (see *paragraph 2.12*).

3.22 Any covert activity should be strictly limited to that necessary to test the ability of the eye-witness to identify the suspect as the person they saw on the relevant previous occasion.

3.23 The identification officer may arrange for the suspect to be confronted by the eye-witness if none of the options referred to in *paragraphs 3.5* to *3.10* or *3.21* are practicable. A "confrontation" is when the suspect is directly confronted by the eye-witness. A confrontation does not require the suspect's consent. Confrontations must be carried out in accordance with Annex D.

3.24 Requirements for information to be given to, or sought from, a suspect or for the suspect to be given an opportunity to view images before they are shown to an eye-witness, do not apply if the suspect's lack of co-operation prevents the necessary action.

(d) Documentation

3.25 A record shall be made of the video identification, identification parade, group identification or confrontation on forms provided for the purpose.

3.26 If the identification officer considers it is not practicable to hold a video identification or identification parade requested by the suspect, the reasons shall be recorded and explained to the suspect.

3.27 A record shall be made of a person's failure or refusal to co-operate in a video identification, identification parade or group identification and, if applicable, of the grounds for obtaining images in accordance with *paragraph 3.20.*

(e) Not used

3.28 *Not used.*

3.29 *Not used.*

(f) Destruction and retention of photographs taken or used in eye-witness identification procedures

3.30 PACE, section 64A, see *paragraph 5.12*, provides powers to take photographs of suspects and allows these photographs to be used or disclosed only for purposes related to the prevention or detection of crime, the investigation of offences or the conduct of prosecutions by, or on behalf of, police or other law enforcement and prosecuting authorities inside and outside the United Kingdom or the enforcement of a sentence. After being so used or disclosed, they may be retained but can only be used or disclosed for the same purposes.

3.31 Subject to *paragraph 3.33,* the photographs (and all negatives and copies), of suspects *not* taken in accordance with the provisions in *paragraph 5.12* which are taken for the purposes of, or in connection with, the identification procedures in *paragraphs 3.5* to *3.10, 3.21 or 3.23* must be destroyed unless the suspect:

(a) is charged with, or informed they may be prosecuted for, a recordable offence;

(b) is prosecuted for a recordable offence;

(c) is cautioned for a recordable offence or given a warning or reprimand in accordance with the Crime and Disorder Act 1998 for a recordable offence; or

(d) gives informed consent, in writing, for the photograph or images to be retained for purposes described in *paragraph 3.30.*

3.32 When *paragraph 3.31* requires the destruction of any photograph, the person must be given an opportunity to witness the destruction or to have a certificate confirming the destruction if they request one within five days of being informed that the destruction is required.

3.33 Nothing in *paragraph 3.31* affects any separate requirement under the Criminal Procedure and Investigations Act 1996 to retain material in connection with criminal investigations.

Part (B) Recognition by controlled showing of films, photographs and images

3.34 This Part of this section applies when, for the purposes of obtaining evidence of recognition, arrangements are made for a person, including a police officer, who is not an eye-witness (see *Note 3AA)*:

(a) to view a film, photograph or any other visual medium; and

(b) on the occasion of the viewing, to be asked whether they recognise anyone whose image is shown in the material as someone who is known to them.

The arrangements for such viewings may be made by the officer in charge of the relevant investigation. Although there is no requirement for the identification officer to make the arrangements or to be consulted about the arrangements, nothing prevents this. See *Notes 3AA* and *3G*.

3.35 To provide safeguards against mistaken recognition and to avoid any possibility of collusion, on the occasion of the viewing, the arrangements should ensure:

(a) that the films, photographs and other images are shown on an individual basis;

(b) that any person who views the material;

(i) is unable to communicate with any other individual to whom the material has been, or is to be, shown;

(ii) is not reminded of any photograph or description of any individual whose image is shown or given any other indication as to the identity of any such individual;

(iii) is not be told whether a previous witness has recognised any one;

(c) that immediately before a person views the material, they are told that:

   (i) an individual who is known to them may, or may not, appear in the material they are shown and that if they do not recognise anyone, they should say so;

   (ii) at any point, they may ask to see a particular part of the material frozen for them to study and there is no limit on how many times they can view the whole or any part or parts of the material; and

(d) that the person who views the material is not asked to make any decision as to whether they recognise anyone whose image they have seen as someone known to them until they have seen the whole of the material at least twice, unless the officer in charge of the viewing decides that because of the number of images the person has been invited to view, it would not be reasonable to ask them to view the whole of the material for a second time. A record of this decision must be included in the record that is made in accordance with *paragraph 3.36.*

(see *Note 3G*).

3.36 A record of the circumstances and conditions under which the person is given an opportunity to recognise an individual must be made and the record must include:

(a) whether the person knew or was given information concerning the name or identity of any suspect;

(b) what the person has been told *before* the viewing about the offence, the person(s) depicted in the images or the offender and by whom;

(c) how and by whom the witness was asked to view the image or look at the individual;

(d) whether the viewing was alone or with others and if with others, the reason for it;

(e) the arrangements under which the person viewed the film or saw the individual and by whom those arrangements were made;

(f) subject to *paragraph 2.18*, the name and rank of the officer responsible for deciding that the viewing arrangements should be made in accordance with this Part;

(g) the date time and place images were viewed or further viewed or the individual was seen;

(h) the times between which the images were viewed or the individual was seen;

(i) how the viewing of images or sighting of the individual was controlled and by whom;

(j) whether the person was familiar with the location shown in any images or the place where they saw the individual and if so, why;

(k) whether or not, on this occasion, the person claims to recognise any image shown, or any individual seen, as being someone known to them, and if they do:

   (i) the reason;

   (ii) the words of recognition;

   (iii) any expressions of doubt; and

   (iv) what features of the image or the individual triggered the recognition.

3.37 The record required under *paragraph 3.36* may be made by the person who views the image or sees the individual and makes the recognition; and if applicable, by the officer or police staff in charge of showing the images to that person or in charge of the conditions under which that person sees the individual. The person must be asked to read and check the completed record and as applicable, confirm that it is correctly and accurately reflects the part they played in the viewing (see *Note 3H*).

Part (C) Recognition by ***uncontrolled*** *viewing of films, photographs and images*

3.38 This Part applies when, for the purpose of identifying and tracing suspects, films and photographs of incidents or other images are:

(a) shown to the public (which may include police officers and police staff as well as members of the public) through the national or local media or any social media networking site; or

(b) circulated through local or national police communication systems for viewing by police officers and police staff; and

the viewing is not formally controlled and supervised as set out in Part B.

3.39 A copy of the relevant material released to the national or local media for showing as described in sub-paragraph 3.38(a), shall be kept. The suspect or their solicitor shall be allowed to view such material before any eye-witness identification procedure under *paragraphs 3.5* to *3.10*, *3.21* or *3.23* of Part A are carried out, provided it is practicable and would not unreasonably delay the investigation. This paragraph does not affect any separate requirement under the Criminal Procedure and Investigations Act 1996 to retain material in connection with criminal investigations that might apply to *sub-paragraphs 3.38(a)* and *(b)*.

3.40 Each eye-witness involved in any eye-witness identification procedure under *paragraphs 3.5* to *3.10*, *3.21* or *3.23* shall be asked, *after they have taken part*, whether they have seen any film, photograph or image relating to the offence or any description of the suspect which has been broadcast or published as described in *paragraph 3.38(a)* and their reply recorded. If they have, they should be asked to give details of the circumstances and subject to the eye-witness's recollection, the record described in *paragraph 3.41* should be completed.

3.41 As soon as practicable after an individual (member of the public, police officer or police staff) indicates in response to a viewing that they may have information relating to the identity and whereabouts of anyone they have seen in that viewing, arrangements should be made to ensure that they are asked to give details of the circumstances and, subject to the individual's recollection, a record of the circumstances and conditions under which the viewing took place is made. This record shall be made in accordance with the provisions of *paragraph 3.36* insofar as they can be applied to the viewing in question (*see* Note 3H).

Notes for guidance

3AA The eye-witness identification procedures in Part A should not be used to test whether a witness can recognise a person as someone they know and would be able to give evidence of recognition along the lines that "On (describe date, time, location and circumstances) I saw an image of an individual who I recognised as AB." In these cases, the procedures in Part B shall apply if the viewing is controlled and the procedure in Part C shall apply if the viewing is not controlled.

3ZA In paragraph 3.5(a)(i), examples of physical changes or differences that the identification officer may wish to consider include hair style and colour, weight, facial hair, wearing or removal of spectacles and tinted contact lenses, facial injuries, tattoos and makeup.

3A Except for the provisions of Annex E, paragraph 1, a police officer who is a witness for the purposes of this part of the Code is subject to the same principles and procedures as a civilian witness.

3B When an eye-witness attending an identification procedure has previously been shown photographs, or been shown or provided with computerised or artist's composite likenesses, or similar likenesses or pictures, it is the officer in charge of the investigation's responsibility to make the identification officer aware of this.

3C *The purpose of paragraph 3.19 is to avoid or reduce delay in arranging identification procedures by enabling the required information and warnings, see sub-paragraphs 3.17(ix) and 3.17(xii), to be given at the earliest opportunity.*

3D *Paragraph 3.21 would apply when a known suspect becomes 'unavailable' and thereby delays or frustrates arrangements for obtaining identification evidence. It also applies when a suspect refuses or fails to take part in a video identification, an identification parade or a group identification, or refuses or fails to take part in the only practicable options from that list. It enables any suitable images of the suspect, moving or still, which are available or can be obtained, to be used in an identification procedure. Examples include images from custody and other CCTV systems and from visually recorded interview records, see Code F Note for Guidance 2D.*

3E *When it is proposed to show photographs to a witness in accordance with Annex E, it is the responsibility of the officer in charge of the investigation to confirm to the officer responsible for supervising and directing the showing, that the first description of the suspect given by that eye-witness has been recorded. If this description has not been recorded, the procedure under Annex E must be postponed, see Annex E paragraph 2.*

3F *The admissibility and value of identification evidence obtained when carrying out the procedure under paragraph 3.2 may be compromised if:*

(a) before a person is identified, the eye-witness' attention is specifically drawn to that person; or

(b) the suspect's identity becomes known before the procedure.

3G *The admissibility and value of evidence of recognition obtained when carrying out the procedures in Part B may be compromised if, before the person is recognised, the witness who has claimed to know them is given or is made, or becomes aware of, information about the person which was not previously known to them personally but which they have purported to rely on to support their claim that the person is in fact known to them.*

3H *It is important that the record referred to in paragraphs 3.36 and 3.41 is made as soon as practicable after the viewing and whilst it is fresh in the mind of the individual who makes the recognition.*

4 Identification by fingerprints and footwear impressions

(A) Taking fingerprints in connection with a criminal investigation

(a) General

4.1 References to 'fingerprints' means any record, produced by any method, of the skin pattern and other physical characteristics or features of a person's:

(i) fingers; or

(ii) palms.

(b) Action

4.2 A person's fingerprints may be taken in connection with the investigation of an offence only with their consent or if *paragraph 4.3* applies. If the person is at a police station, consent must be in writing.

4.3 PACE, section 61, provides powers to take fingerprints without consent from any person aged ten or over as follows:

(a) under *section 61(3)*, from a person detained at a police station in consequence of being arrested for a recordable offence, see *Note 4A*, if they have not had their fingerprints taken in the course of the investigation of the offence unless those previously taken fingerprints are not a complete set or some or all of those fingerprints are not of sufficient quality to allow satisfactory analysis, comparison or matching.

(b) under *section 61(4)*, from a person detained at a police station who has been charged with a recordable offence, see *Note 4A*, or informed they will be reported for such an offence if they have not had their fingerprints taken in the course of the investigation of the offence unless those previously taken fingerprints are not a complete set or some or all of those fingerprints are not of sufficient quality to allow satisfactory analysis, comparison or matching.

(c) under *section 61(4A)*, from a person who has been bailed to appear at a court or police station if the person:

(i) has answered to bail for a person whose fingerprints were taken previously and there are reasonable grounds for believing they are not the same person; or

(ii) who has answered to bail claims to be a different person from a person whose fingerprints were previously taken;

and in either case, the court or an officer of inspector rank or above, authorises the fingerprints to be taken at the court or police station (an inspector's authority may be given in writing or orally and confirmed in writing, as soon as practicable);

(ca) under *section 61(5A)* from a person who has been arrested for a recordable offence and released if the person:

(i) is on bail and has not had their fingerprints taken in the course of the investigation of the offence, or;

(ii) has had their fingerprints taken in the course of the investigation of the offence, but they do not constitute a complete set or some, or all, of the fingerprints are not of sufficient quality to allow satisfactory analysis, comparison or matching.

(cb) under *section 61(5B)* from a person not detained at a police station who has been charged with a recordable offence or informed they will be reported for such an offence if:

(i) they have not had their fingerprints taken in the course of the investigation; or

(ii) their fingerprints have been taken in the course of the investigation of the offence but either:

- they do not constitute a complete set or some, or all, of the fingerprints are not of sufficient quality to allow satisfactory analysis, comparison or matching; or

- the investigation was discontinued but subsequently resumed and, before the resumption, their fingerprints were destroyed pursuant to section 63D(3).

(d) under *section 61(6)*, from a person who has been:

(i) convicted of a recordable offence; or

(ii) given a caution in respect of a recordable offence (see Note 4A) which, at the time of the caution, the person admitted;

if, since being convicted or cautioned:

- their fingerprints have not been taken; or
- their fingerprints which have been taken do not constitute a complete set or some, or all, of the fingerprints are not of sufficient quality to allow satisfactory analysis, comparison or matching;

and in either case, an officer of inspector rank or above is satisfied that taking the fingerprints is necessary to assist in the prevention or detection of crime and authorises the taking;

(e) under *section 61(6A)* from a person a constable reasonably suspects is committing or attempting to commit, or has committed or attempted to commit, any offence if either:

(i) the person's name is unknown to, and cannot be readily ascertained by, the constable; or

(ii) the constable has reasonable grounds for doubting whether a name given by the person as their name is their real name.

Note: fingerprints taken under this power are not regarded as having been taken in the course of the investigation of an offence.

[See *Note 4C*]

(f) under *section 61(6D)* from a person who has been convicted outside England and Wales of an offence which if committed in England and Wales would be a qualifying offence as defined by PACE, section 65A (see Note 4AB) if:

(i) the person's fingerprints have not been taken previously under this power or their fingerprints have been so taken on a previous occasion but they do not constitute a complete set or some, or all, of the fingerprints are not of sufficient quality to allow satisfactory analysis, comparison or matching; and

(ii) a police officer of inspector rank or above is satisfied that taking fingerprints is necessary to assist in the prevention or detection of crime and authorises them to be taken.

4.4 PACE, section 63A(4) and Schedule 2A provide powers to:

(a) make a requirement (in accordance with Annex G) for a person to attend a police station to have their fingerprints taken in the exercise of one of the following powers (described in *paragraph 4.3* above) within certain periods as follows:

(i) *section 61(5A)* – Persons arrested for a recordable offence and released, see *paragraph 4.3(ca)*: In the case of a person whose fingerprints were taken in the course of the investigation but those fingerprints do not constitute a complete set or some, or all, of the fingerprints are not of sufficient quality, the requirement may not be made more than six months from the day the investigating officer was informed that the fingerprints previously taken were incomplete or below standard. In the case of a person whose fingerprints were destroyed prior to the resumption of the investigation, the requirement may not be made more than six months from the day on which the investigation resumed.

(ii) *section 61(5B)* – Persons not detained at a police station charged etc. with a recordable offence, see *paragraph 4.3(cb)*: The requirement may not be made more than six months from:

- the day the person was charged or informed that they would be reported, if fingerprints have not been taken in the course of the investigation of the offence; or
- the day the investigating officer was informed that the fingerprints previously taken were incomplete or below standard, if fingerprints have been taken in the course of the investigation but those fingerprints do not constitute a complete set or some, or all, of the fingerprints are not of sufficient quality; or
- the day on which the investigation was resumed, in the case of a person whose fingerprints were destroyed prior to the resumption of the investigation.

(iii) *section 61(6)* – Persons convicted or cautioned for a recordable offence in England and Wales, see *paragraph 4.3(d)*: Where the offence for which the person was convicted or cautioned is a qualifying offence (see *Note 4AB*), there is no time limit for the exercise of this power. Where the conviction or caution is for a recordable offence which is not a qualifying offence, the requirement may not be made more than two years from:

- in the case of a person who has not had their fingerprints taken since the conviction or caution, the day on which the person was convicted or cautioned, or, if later, the day on which Schedule 2A came into force (March 7, 2011), ; or
- in the case of a person whose fingerprints have been taken in the course of the investigation but those fingerprints do not constitute a complete set or some, or all, of the fingerprints are not of sufficient quality, the day on which an officer from the force investigating the offence was informed that the fingerprints previously taken were incomplete or below standard, or, if later, the day on which Schedule 2A came into force (March 7, 2011).

(iv) *section 61(6D)* – A person who has been convicted of a qualifying offence (see *Note 4AB*) outside England and Wales, see paragraph 4.3(g): There is no time limit for making the requirement.

Note: A person who has had their fingerprints taken under any of the powers in section 61 mentioned in *paragraph 4.3* on two occasions in relation to any offence may not be required under Schedule 2A to attend a police station for their fingerprints to be taken again under section 61 in relation to that offence, unless authorised by an officer of inspector rank or above. The fact of the authorisation and the reasons for giving it must be recorded as soon as practicable.

(b) arrest, without warrant, a person who fails to comply with the requirement.

4.5 A person's fingerprints may be taken, as above, electronically.

4.6 Reasonable force may be used, if necessary, to take a person's fingerprints without their consent under the powers as in *paragraphs 4.3* and *4.4*.

4.7 Before any fingerprints are taken:

(a) without consent under any power mentioned in *paragraphs 4.3* and *4.4* above, the person must be informed of:

(i) the reason their fingerprints are to be taken;

(ii) the power under which they are to be taken; and

(iii) the fact that the relevant authority has been given if any power mentioned in *paragraph 4.3(c), (d)* or *(f)* applies

(b) with or without consent at a police station or elsewhere, the person must be informed:

(i) that their fingerprints may be subject of a speculative search against other fingerprints, see *Note 4B*; and

(ii) that their fingerprints may be retained in accordance with *Annex F, Part (a)* unless they were taken under the power mentioned in paragraph 4.3(e) when they must be destroyed after they have being checked (See *Note 4C*).

(c) Documentation

4.8A A record must be made as soon as practicable after the fingerprints are taken, of:

- the matters in paragraph 4.7(a)(i) to (iii) and the fact that the person has been informed of those matters; and
- the fact that the person has been informed of the matters in paragraph 4.7(b)(i) and (ii).

The record must be made in the person's custody record if they are detained at a police station when the fingerprints are taken.

4.8 If force is used, a record shall be made of the circumstances and those present.

4.9 Not used

(B) Not used

4.10 *Not used*

4.11 *Not used*

4.12 *Not used*

4.13 *Not used*

4.14 *Not used*

4.15 *Not used*

(C) Taking footwear impressions in connection with a criminal investigation

(a) Action

4.16 Impressions of a person's footwear may be taken in connection with the investigation of an offence only with their consent or if *paragraph 4.17* applies. If the person is at a police station consent must be in writing.

4.17 PACE, section 61A, provides power for a police officer to take footwear impressions without consent from any person over the age of ten years who is detained at a police station:

(a) in consequence of being arrested for a recordable offence, see *Note 4A*; or if the detainee has been charged with a recordable offence, or informed they will be reported for such an offence; and

(b) the detainee has not had an impression of their footwear taken in the course of the investigation of the offence unless the previously taken impression is not complete or is not of sufficient quality to allow satisfactory analysis, comparison or matching (whether in the case in question or generally).

4.18 Reasonable force may be used, if necessary, to take a footwear impression from a detainee without consent under the power in *paragraph 4.17*.

4.19 Before any footwear impression is taken with, or without, consent as above, the person must be informed:

(a) of the reason the impression is to be taken;

(b) that the impression may be retained and may be subject of a speculative search against other impressions, see *Note 4B*, unless destruction of the impression is required in accordance with *Annex F, Part B*.

(b) Documentation

4.20 A record must be made, as soon as possible, of the reason for taking a person's footwear impressions without consent. If force is used, a record shall be made of the circumstances and those present.

4.21 A record shall be made when a person has been informed under the terms of *paragraph 4.19(b)*, of the possibility that their footwear impressions may be subject of a speculative search.

Notes for guidance

4A References to 'recordable offences' in this Code relate to those offences for which convictions or cautions may be recorded in national police records. See PACE, section 27(4). The recordable offences current at the time when this Code was prepared, are any offences which carry a sentence of imprisonment on conviction (irrespective of the period, or the age of the offender or actual sentence passed) as well as the non-imprisonable offences under the Vagrancy Act 1824 sections 3 and 4 (begging and persistent begging), the Street Offences Act 1959, section 1 (loitering or soliciting for purposes of prostitution), the Road Traffic Act 1988, section 25 (tampering with motor vehicles), the Criminal Justice and Public Order Act 1994, section 167 (touting for hire car services) and others listed in the National Police Records (Recordable Offences) Regulations 2000 as amended.

4AB A qualifying offence is one of the offences specified in PACE, section 65A. These include offences which involve the use or threat of violence or unlawful force against persons, sexual offences, offences against children and other offences, for example:

- *murder, false imprisonment, kidnapping contrary to Common law*
- *manslaughter, conspiracy to murder, threats to kill, wounding with intent to cause grievous bodily harm (GBH), causing GBH and assault occasioning actual bodily harm contrary to the Offences Against the Person Act 1861;*
- *criminal possession or use of firearms contrary to sections 16 to 18 of the Firearms Act 1968;*
- *robbery, burglary and aggravated burglary contrary to sections 8, 9 or 10 of the Theft Act 1968 or an offence under section 12A of that Act involving an accident which caused a person's death;*
- *criminal damage required to be charged as arson contrary to section 1 of the Criminal Damage Act 1971;*
- *taking, possessing and showing indecent photographs of children contrary to section 1 of the Protection of Children Act 1978;*
- *rape, sexual assault, child sex offences, exposure and other offences contrary to the Sexual Offences Act 2003.*

4B Fingerprints, footwear impressions or a DNA sample (and the information derived from it) taken from a person arrested on suspicion of being involved in a recordable offence, or charged with such an offence, or informed they will be reported for such an offence, may be subject of a speculative search. This means the fingerprints, footwear impressions or DNA sample may be checked against other fingerprints, footwear impressions and DNA records held by, or on behalf of, the police and other law enforcement authorities in, or outside, the UK, or held in connection with, or as a result of, an investigation of an offence inside or outside the UK.

4C The power under section 61(6A) of PACE described in paragraph 4.3(e) allows fingerprints of a suspect who has not been arrested, and whose name is not known or cannot be ascertained, or who gave a doubtful name, to be taken in connection with any offence (whether recordable or not) using a mobile device and then checked on the street against the database containing the national fingerprint collection. Fingerprints taken under this power cannot be retained after they have been checked. The results may make an arrest for the suspected offence based on the name condition unnecessary (See Code G paragraph 2.9(a)) and enable the offence to be disposed of without arrest, for example, by summons/charging by post, penalty notice or words of advice. If arrest for a non-recordable offence is necessary for any other reasons, this power may also be exercised at the station. Before the power is exercised, the officer should:

- *inform the person of the nature of the suspected offence and why they are suspected of committing it.*
- *give them a reasonable opportunity to establish their real name before deciding that their name is unknown and cannot be readily ascertained or that there are reasonable grounds to doubt that a name they have given is their real name.*
- *as applicable, inform the person of the reason why their name is not known and cannot be readily ascertained or of the grounds for doubting that a name they have given is their real name, including, for example, the reason why a particular document the person has produced to verify their real name, is not sufficient.*

4D Not used.

5 Examinations to establish identity and the taking of photographs

(A) Detainees at police stations

(a) Searching or examination of detainees at police stations

5.1 PACE, section 54A(1), allows a detainee at a police station to be searched or examined or both, to establish:

(a) whether they have any marks, features or injuries that would tend to identify them as a person involved in the commission of an offence and to photograph any identifying marks, see *paragraph 5.5*; or

(b) their identity, see *Note 5A*.

A person detained at a police station to be searched under a stop and search power, see Code A, is not a detainee for the purposes of these powers.

5.2 A search and/or examination to find marks under section 54A (1) (a) may be carried out without the detainee's consent, see *paragraph 2.12*, only if authorised by an officer of at least inspector rank when consent has been withheld or it is not practicable to obtain consent, see *Note 5D.*

5.3 A search or examination to establish a suspect's identity under section 54A (1) (b) may be carried out without the detainee's consent, see *paragraph 2.12*, only if authorised by an officer of at least inspector rank when the detainee has refused to identify themselves or the authorising officer has reasonable grounds for suspecting the person is not who they claim to be.

5.4 Any marks that assist in establishing the detainee's identity, or their identification as a person involved in the commission of an offence, are identifying marks. Such marks may be photographed with the detainee's consent, see *paragraph 2.12*; or without their consent if it is withheld or it is not practicable to obtain it, see *Note 5D.*

5.5 A detainee may only be searched, examined and photographed under section 54A, by a police officer of the same sex.

5.6 Any photographs of identifying marks, taken under section 54A, may be used or disclosed only for purposes related to the prevention or detection of crime, the investigation of offences or the conduct of prosecutions by, or on behalf of, police or other law enforcement and prosecuting authorities inside, and outside, the UK. After being so used or disclosed, the photograph may be retained but must not be used or disclosed except for these purposes, see *Note 5B.*

5.7 The powers, as in *paragraph 5.1,* do not affect any separate requirement under the Criminal Procedure and Investigations Act 1996 to retain material in connection with criminal investigations.

5.8 Authority for the search and/or examination for the purposes of *paragraphs 5.2* and *5.3* may be given orally or in writing. If given orally, the authorising officer must confirm it in writing as soon as practicable. A separate authority is required for each purpose which applies.

5.9 If it is established a person is unwilling to co-operate sufficiently to enable a search and/or examination to take place or a suitable photograph to be taken, an officer may use reasonable force to:

(a) search and/or examine a detainee without their consent; and

(b) photograph any identifying marks without their consent.

5.10 The thoroughness and extent of any search or examination carried out in accordance with the powers in section 54A must be no more than the officer considers necessary to achieve the required purpose. Any search or examination which involves the removal of more than the person's outer clothing shall be conducted in accordance with Code C, Annex A, paragraph 11.

5.11 An intimate search may not be carried out under the powers in section 54A.

(b) Photographing detainees at police stations and other persons elsewhere than at a police station

5.12 Under PACE, section 64A, an officer may photograph:

(a) any person whilst they are detained at a police station; and

(b) any person who is elsewhere than at a police station and who has been:

(i) arrested by a constable for an offence;

(ii) taken into custody by a constable after being arrested for an offence by a person other than a constable;

(iii) made subject to a requirement to wait with a community support officer under paragraph 2(3) or (3B) of Schedule 4 to the Police Reform Act 2002;

(iiia) given a direction by a constable under section 27 of the Violent Crime Reduction Act 2006.

(iv) given a penalty notice by a constable in uniform under Chapter 1 of Part 1 of the Criminal Justice and Police Act 2001, a penalty notice by a constable under section 444A of the Education Act 1996, or a fixed penalty notice by a constable in uniform under section 54 of the Road Traffic Offenders Act 1988;

(v) given a notice in relation to a relevant fixed penalty offence (within the meaning of paragraph 1 of Schedule 4 to the Police Reform Act 2002) by a community support officer by virtue of a designation applying that paragraph to him;

(vi) given a notice in relation to a relevant fixed penalty offence (within the meaning of paragraph 1 of Schedule 5 to the Police Reform Act 2002) by an accredited person by virtue of accreditation specifying that that paragraph applies to him; or

(vii) given a direction to leave and not return to a specified location for up to 48 hours by a police constable (under section 27 of the Violent Crime Reduction Act 2006).

5.12A Photographs taken under PACE, section 64A:

(a) may be taken with the person's consent, or without their consent if consent is withheld or it is not practicable to obtain their consent, see *Note 5E*; and

(b) may be used or disclosed only for purposes related to the prevention or detection of crime, the investigation of offences or the conduct of prosecutions by, or on behalf of, police or other law enforcement and prosecuting authorities inside and outside the United Kingdom or the enforcement of any sentence or order made by a court when dealing with an offence. After being so used or disclosed, they may be retained but can only be used or disclosed for the same purposes. See *Note 5B.*

5.13 The officer proposing to take a detainee's photograph may, for this purpose, require the person to remove any item or substance worn on, or over, all, or any part of, their head or face. If they do not comply with such a requirement, the officer may remove the item or substance.

5.14 If it is established the detainee is unwilling to co-operate sufficiently to enable a suitable photograph to be taken and it is not reasonably practicable to take the photograph covertly, an officer may use reasonable force, see *Note 5F.*

(a) to take their photograph without their consent; and

(b) for the purpose of taking the photograph, remove any item or substance worn on, or over, all, or any part of, the person's head or face which they have failed to remove when asked.

5.15 For the purposes of this Code, a photograph may be obtained without the person's consent by making a copy of an image of them taken at any time on a camera system installed anywhere in the police station.

(c) Information to be given

5.16 When a person is searched, examined or photographed under the provisions as in *paragraph 5.1* and *5.12*, or their photograph obtained as in *paragraph 5.15*, they must be informed of the:

(a) purpose of the search, examination or photograph;

(b) grounds on which the relevant authority, if applicable, has been given; and

(c) purposes for which the photograph may be used, disclosed or retained.

This information must be given before the search or examination commences or the photograph is taken, except if the photograph is:

(i) to be taken covertly;

(ii) obtained as in *paragraph 5.15*, in which case the person must be informed as soon as practicable after the photograph is taken or obtained.

(d) Documentation

5.17 A record must be made when a detainee is searched, examined, or a photograph of the person, or any identifying marks found on them, are taken. The record must include the:

(a) identity, subject to paragraph 2.18, of the officer carrying out the search, examination or taking the photograph;

(b) purpose of the search, examination or photograph and the outcome;

(c) detainee's consent to the search, examination or photograph, or the reason the person was searched, examined or photographed without consent;

(d) giving of any authority as in *paragraphs 5.2* and *5.3*, the grounds for giving it and the authorising officer.

5.18 If force is used when searching, examining or taking a photograph in accordance with this section, a record shall be made of the circumstances and those present.

(B) Persons at police stations not detained

5.19 When there are reasonable grounds for suspecting the involvement of a person in a criminal offence, but that person is at a police station **voluntarily** and not detained, the provisions of *paragraphs 5.1* to *5.18* should apply, subject to the modifications in the following paragraphs.

5.20 References to the 'person being detained' and to the powers mentioned in *paragraph 5.1* which apply only to detainees at police stations shall be omitted.

5.21 Force may not be used to:

(a) search and/or examine the person to:

(i) discover whether they have any marks that would tend to identify them as a person involved in the commission of an offence; or

(ii) establish their identity, see *Note 5A*;

(b) take photographs of any identifying marks, see *paragraph 5.4*; or

(c) take a photograph of the person.

5.22 Subject to *paragraph 5.24*, the photographs of persons or of their identifying marks which are not taken in accordance with the provisions mentioned in *paragraphs 5.1* or *5.12*, must be destroyed (together with any negatives and copies) unless the person:

(a) is charged with, or informed they may be prosecuted for, a recordable offence;

(b) is prosecuted for a recordable offence;

(c) is cautioned for a recordable offence or given a warning or reprimand in accordance with the Crime and Disorder Act 1998 for a recordable offence; or

(d) gives informed consent, in writing, for the photograph or image to be retained as in *paragraph 5.6*.

5.23 When *paragraph 5.22* requires the destruction of any photograph, the person must be given an opportunity to witness the destruction or to have a certificate confirming the destruction provided they so request the certificate within five days of being informed the destruction is required.

5.24 Nothing in *paragraph 5.22* affects any separate requirement under the Criminal Procedure and Investigations Act 1996 to retain material in connection with criminal investigations.

Notes for guidance

5A The conditions under which fingerprints may be taken to assist in establishing a person's identity, are described in Section 4.

5B Examples of purposes related to the prevention or detection of crime, the investigation of offences or the conduct of prosecutions include:

(a) checking the photograph against other photographs held in records or in connection with, or as a result of, an investigation of an offence to establish whether the person is liable to arrest for other offences;

(b) when the person is arrested at the same time as other people, or at a time when it is likely that other people will be arrested, using the photograph to help establish who was arrested, at what time and where;

(c) when the real identity of the person is not known and cannot be readily ascertained or there are reasonable grounds for doubting a name and other personal details given by the person, are their real name and personal details. In these circumstances, using or disclosing the photograph to help to establish or verify their real identity or determine whether they are liable to arrest for some other offence, e.g. by checking it against other photographs held in records or in connection with, or as a result of, an investigation of an offence;

(d) when it appears any identification procedure in section 3 may need to be arranged for which the person's photograph would assist;

(e) when the person's release without charge may be required, and if the release is:

(i) on bail to appear at a police station, using the photograph to help verify the person's identity when they answer their bail and if the person does not answer their bail, to assist in arresting them; or

(ii) without bail, using the photograph to help verify their identity or assist in locating them for the purposes of serving them with a summons to appear at court in criminal proceedings;

(f) when the person has answered to bail at a police station and there are reasonable grounds for doubting they are the person who was previously granted bail, using the photograph to help establish or verify their identity;

(g) when the person arrested on a warrant claims to be a different person from the person named on the warrant and a photograph would help to confirm or disprove their claim;

(h) when the person has been charged with, reported for, or convicted of, a recordable offence and their photograph is not already on record as a result of (a) to (f) or their photograph is on record but their appearance has changed since it was taken and the person has not yet been released or brought before a court.

5C There is no power to arrest a person convicted of a recordable offence solely to take their photograph. The power to take photographs in this section applies only where the person is in custody as a result of the exercise of another power, e.g. arrest for fingerprinting under PACE, Schedule 2A, paragraph 17.

5D *Examples of when it would not be practicable to obtain a detainee's consent, see paragraph 2.12, to a search, examination or the taking of a photograph of an identifying mark include:*

- *(a) when the person is drunk or otherwise unfit to give consent;*
- *(b) when there are reasonable grounds to suspect that if the person became aware a search or examination was to take place or an identifying mark was to be photographed, they would take steps to prevent this happening, e.g. by violently resisting, covering or concealing the mark etc and it would not otherwise be possible to carry out the search or examination or to photograph any identifying mark;*
- *(c) in the case of a juvenile, if the parent or guardian cannot be contacted in sufficient time to allow the search or examination to be carried out or the photograph to be taken.*

5E *Examples of when it would not be practicable to obtain the person's consent, see paragraph 2.12, to a photograph being taken include:*

- *(a) when the person is drunk or otherwise unfit to give consent;*
- *(b) when there are reasonable grounds to suspect that if the person became aware a photograph, suitable to be used or disclosed for the use and disclosure described in paragraph 5.6, was to be taken, they would take steps to prevent it being taken, e.g. by violently resisting, covering or distorting their face etc, and it would not otherwise be possible to take a suitable photograph;*
- *(c) when, in order to obtain a suitable photograph, it is necessary to take it covertly; and*
- *(d) in the case of a juvenile, if the parent or guardian cannot be contacted in sufficient time to allow the photograph to be taken.*

5F *The use of reasonable force to take the photograph of a suspect elsewhere than at a police station must be carefully considered. In order to obtain a suspect's consent and co-operation to remove an item of religious headwear to take their photograph, a constable should consider whether in the circumstances of the situation the removal of the headwear and the taking of the photograph should be by an officer of the same sex as the person. It would be appropriate for these actions to be conducted out of public view (see paragraph 1.1 and Note 1A).*

6 Identification by body samples and impressions

(A) General

6.1 References to:

(a) an 'intimate sample' mean a dental impression or sample of blood, semen or any other tissue fluid, urine, or pubic hair, or a swab taken from any part of a person's genitals or from a person's body orifice other than the mouth;

(b) a 'non-intimate sample' means:

(i) a sample of hair, other than pubic hair, which includes hair plucked with the root, see *Note 6A*;

(ii) a sample taken from a nail or from under a nail;

(iii) a swab taken from any part of a person's body other than a part from which a swab taken would be an intimate sample;

(iv) saliva;

(v) a skin impression which means any record, other than a fingerprint, which is a record, in any form and produced by any method, of the skin pattern and other physical characteristics or features of the whole, or any part of, a person's foot or of any other part of their body.

(B) Action

(a) Intimate samples

6.2 PACE, section 62, provides that intimate samples may be taken under:

(a) section 62(1), from a person in police detention only:

(i) if a police officer of inspector rank or above has reasonable grounds to believe such an impression or sample will tend to confirm or disprove the suspect's involvement in a recordable offence, see *Note 4A*, and gives authorisation for a sample to be taken; and

(ii) with the suspect's written consent;

(b) section 62(1A), from a person not in police detention but from whom two or more non-intimate samples have been taken in the course of an investigation of an offence and the samples, though suitable, have proved insufficient if:

(i) a police officer of inspector rank or above authorises it to be taken; and

(ii) the person concerned gives their written consent. See *Notes 6B* and *6C*

(c) section 62(2A), from a person convicted outside England and Wales of an offence which if committed in England and Wales would be qualifying offence as defined by PACE, section 65A (see *Note 4AB*) from whom two or more non-intimate samples taken under section 63(3E) (see *paragraph 6.6(h)* have proved insufficient if:

(i) a police officer of inspector rank or above is satisfied that taking the sample is necessary to assist in the prevention or detection of crime and authorises it to be taken; and

(ii) the person concerned gives their written consent.

6.2A PACE, section 63A(4) and Schedule 2A provide powers to:

(a) make a requirement (in accordance with Annex G) for a person to attend a police station to have an intimate sample taken in the exercise of one of the following powers (see *paragraph 6.2*) :

(i) *section 62(1A)* – Persons from whom two or more non-intimate samples have been taken and proved to be insufficient, see paragraph 6.2(b): There is no time limit for making the requirement.

(ii) *section 62(2A)* – Persons convicted outside England and Wales from whom two or more non-intimate samples taken under section 63(3E) (see paragraph 6.6(g)have proved insufficient, see *paragraph 6.2(c)*: There is no time limit for making the requirement.

(b) arrest without warrant a person who fails to comply with the requirement

6.3 Before a suspect is asked to provide an intimate sample, they must be:

(a) informed:

(i) of the reason, including the nature of the suspected offence (except if taken under paragraph 6.2(c) from a person convicted outside England and Wales.

(ii) that authorisation has been given and the provisions under which given;

(iii) that a sample taken at a police station may be subject of a speculative search;

(b) warned that if they refuse without good cause their refusal may harm their case if it comes to trial, see *Note 6D*. If the suspect is in police detention and not legally represented, they must also be reminded of their entitlement to have free legal advice, see Code C, *paragraph 6.5*, and the reminder noted in the custody record. If *paragraph 6.2(b)* applies and the person is attending a station voluntarily, their entitlement to free legal advice as in Code C, *paragraph 3.21* shall be explained to them.

6.4 Dental impressions may only be taken by a registered dentist. Other intimate samples, except for samples of urine, may only be taken by a registered medical practitioner or registered nurse or registered paramedic.

(b) Non-intimate samples

6.5 A non-intimate sample may be taken from a detainee only with their written consent or if *paragraph 6.6* applies.

6.6 A non-intimate sample may be taken from a person without the appropriate consent in the following circumstances:

(a) under *section 63(2A)* from a person who is in police detention as a consequence of being arrested for a recordable offence and who has not had a non-intimate sample of the same type and from the same part of the body taken in the course of the investigation of the offence by the police or they have had such a sample taken but it proved insufficient.

(b) Under *section 63(3)* from a person who is being held in custody by the police on the authority of a court if an officer of at least the rank of inspector authorises it to be taken. An authorisation may be given:

(i) if the authorising officer has reasonable grounds for suspecting the person of involvement in a recordable offence and for believing that the sample will tend to confirm or disprove that involvement, and

(ii) in writing or orally and confirmed in writing, as soon as practicable;

but an authorisation may not be given to take from the same part of the body a further non-intimate sample consisting of a skin impression unless the previously taken impression proved insufficient

(c) under *section 63(3ZA)* from a person who has been arrested for a recordable offence and released if:

(i) in the case of a person who is on bail, they have not had a sample of the same type and from the same part of the body taken in the course of the investigation of the offence, or;

(ii) in any case, the person has had such a sample taken in the course of the investigation of the offence, but either:

- it was not suitable or proved insufficient; or

- the investigation was discontinued but subsequently resumed and before the resumption, any DNA profile derived from the sample was destroyed and the sample itself was destroyed pursuant to section 63R(4), (5) or (12).

(d) under *section 63(3A)*, from a person (whether or not in police detention or held in custody by the police on the authority of a court) who has been charged with a recordable offence or informed they will be reported for such an offence if the person:

(i) has not had a non-intimate sample taken from them in the course of the investigation of the offence; or

(ii) has had a sample so taken, but it was not suitable or proved insufficient, see *Note 6B*; or

(iii) has had a sample taken in the course of the investigation of the offence and the sample has been destroyed and in proceedings relating to that offence there is a dispute as to whether a DNA profile relevant to the proceedings was derived from the destroyed sample.

(e) under *section 63(3B)*, from a person who has been:

(i) convicted of a recordable offence; or

(ii) given a caution in respect of a recordable offence which, at the time of the caution, the person admitted;

if, since their conviction or caution a non-intimate sample has not been taken from them or a sample which has been taken since then was not suitable or proved insufficient and in either case, an officer of inspector rank or above, is satisfied that taking the fingerprints is necessary to assist in the prevention or detection of crime and authorises the taking;

(f) under *section 63(3C)* from a person to whom section 2 of the Criminal Evidence (Amendment) Act 1997 applies (persons detained following acquittal on grounds of insanity or finding of unfitness to plead).

(g) under *section 63(3E)* from a person who has been convicted outside England and Wales of an offence which if committed in England and Wales would be a qualifying offence as defined by PACE, section 65A (see *Note 4AB*) if:

(i) a non-intimate sample has not been taken previously under this power or unless a sample was so taken but was not suitable or proved insufficient; and

(ii) a police officer of inspector rank or above is satisfied that taking a sample is necessary to assist in the prevention or detection of crime and authorises it to be taken.

6.6A PACE, *section 63A(4)* and *Schedule 2A* provide powers to:

(a) make a requirement (in accordance with Annex G) for a person to attend a police station to have a non-intimate sample taken in the exercise of one of the following powers (see *paragraph 6.6* above) within certain time limits as follows:

(i) *section 63(3ZA)* – Persons arrested for a recordable offence and released, see paragraph 6.6(c): In the case of a person from whom a non-intimate sample was taken in the course of the investigation but that sample was not suitable or proved insufficient, the requirement may not be made more than six months from the day the investigating officer was informed that the sample previously taken was not suitable or proved insufficient. In the case of a person whose DNA profile and sample was destroyed prior to the resumption of the investigation, the requirement may not be made more than six months from the day on which the investigation resumed.

(ii) *section 63(3A)* – Persons charged etc. with a recordable offence, see paragraph 6.6(d): The requirement may not be made more than six months from:

- the day the person was charged or informed that they would be reported, if a sample has not been taken in the course of the investigation;

- the day the investigating officer was informed that the sample previously taken was not suitable or proved insufficient, if a sample has been taken in the course of the investigation but the sample was not suitable or proved insufficient; or
- the day on which the investigation was resumed, in the case of a person whose DNA profile and sample were destroyed prior to the resumption of the investigation.

(iii) *section 63(3B)* – Person convicted or cautioned for a recordable offence in England and Wales, see paragraph 6.6(e): Where the offence for which the person was convicted etc is also a qualifying offence (see *Note 4AB*), there is no time limit for the exercise of this power. Where the conviction etc was for a recordable offence that is <u>not</u> a qualifying offence, the requirement may not be made more than two years from:

- in the case of a person whose sample has not been taken since they were convicted or cautioned, the day the person was convicted or cautioned, , or, if later. the day Schedule 2A came into force (March 7 2011); or
- in the case of a person whose sample has been taken but was not suitable or proved insufficient, the day an officer from the force investigating the offence was informed that the sample previously taken was not suitable or proved insufficient or, if later, the day Schedule 2A came into force (March 7 2011).

(iv) *section 63(3E)* – A person who has been convicted of qualifying offence (see *Note 4AB*) outside England and Wales, see *paragraph 6.6(h)*: There is no time limit for making the requirement.

Note: A person who has had a non-intimate sample taken under any of the powers in section 63 mentioned in paragraph 6.6 on two occasions in relation to any offence may not be required under Schedule 2A to attend a police station for a sample to be taken again under section 63 in relation to that offence, unless authorised by an officer of inspector rank or above. The fact of the authorisation and the reasons for giving it must be recorded as soon as practicable.

(b) arrest, without warrant, a person who fails to comply with the requirement.

6.7 Reasonable force may be used, if necessary, to take a non-intimate sample from a person without their consent under the powers mentioned in *paragraph 6.6*.

6.8 Before any non-intimate sample is taken:

(a) without consent under any power mentioned in paragraphs 6.6 and 6.6A, the person must be informed of:

(i) the reason for taking the sample;

(ii) the power under which the sample is to be taken;

(iii) the fact that the relevant authority has been given if any power mentioned in *paragraph 6.6(b), (e)* or *(g)* applies, including the nature of the suspected offence (except if taken under *paragraph 6.6(e)* from a person convicted or cautioned, or under *paragraph 6.6(g)* if taken from a person convicted outside England and Wales;

(b) with or without consent at a police station or elsewhere, the person must be informed:

(i) that their sample or information derived from it may be subject of a speculative search against other samples and information derived from them, see *Note 6E* and

(ii) that their sample and the information derived from it may be retained in accordance with Annex F, Part (a).

(c) Removal of clothing

6.9 When clothing needs to be removed in circumstances likely to cause embarrassment to the person, no person of the opposite sex who is not a registered medical practitioner or registered health care professional shall be present, (unless in the case of a juvenile, mentally disordered or mentally vulnerable person, that person specifically requests the presence of an appropriate adult of the opposite sex who is readily available) nor shall anyone whose presence is unnecessary. However, in the case of a juvenile, this is subject to the overriding proviso that such a removal of clothing may take place in the absence of the appropriate adult only if the juvenile signifies in their presence, that they prefer the adult's absence and they agree.

(c) Documentation

6.10 A record must be made as soon as practicable after the sample is taken of:

- The matters in *paragraph 6.8(a)(i)* to *(iii)* and the fact that the person has been informed of those matters; and
- The fact that the person has been informed of the matters in paragraph 6.8(b)(i) and (ii).

6.10A If force is used, a record shall be made of the circumstances and those present.

6.11 A record must be made of a warning given as required by *paragraph 6.3.*

6.12 *Not used*

Notes for guidance

6A *When hair samples are taken for the purpose of DNA analysis (rather than for other purposes such as making a visual match), the suspect should be permitted a reasonable choice as to what part of the body the hairs are taken from. When hairs are plucked, they should be plucked individually, unless the suspect prefers otherwise and no more should be plucked than the person taking them reasonably considers necessary for a sufficient sample.*

6B *(a) An insufficient sample is one which is not sufficient either in quantity or quality to provide information for a particular form of analysis, such as DNA analysis. A sample may also be insufficient if enough information cannot be obtained from it by analysis because of loss, destruction, damage or contamination of the sample or as a result of an earlier, unsuccessful attempt at analysis.*

(b) An unsuitable sample is one which, by its nature, is not suitable for a particular form of analysis.

6C *Nothing in paragraph 6.2 prevents intimate samples being taken for elimination purposes with the consent of the person concerned but the provisions of paragraph 2.12 relating to the role of the appropriate adult, should be applied. Paragraph 6.2(b) does not, however, apply where the non-intimate samples were previously taken under the Terrorism Act 2000, Schedule 8, paragraph 10.*

6D *In warning a person who is asked to provide an intimate sample as in paragraph 6.3, the following form of words may be used:*

> *'You do not have to provide this sample/allow this swab or impression to be taken, but I must warn you that if you refuse without good cause, your refusal may harm your case if it comes to trial.'*

6E *Fingerprints or a DNA sample and the information derived from it taken from a person arrested on suspicion of being involved in a recordable offence, or charged with such an offence, or informed they will be reported for such an offence, may be subject of a speculative search. This means they may be checked against other fingerprints and DNA records held by, or on behalf of, the police and other law enforcement authorities in or outside the UK or held in connection with, or as a result of, an investigation of an offence inside or outside the UK.*

See Annex F regarding the retention and use of fingerprints and samples taken with consent for elimination purposes.

6F *Samples of urine and non-intimate samples taken in accordance with sections 63B and 63C of PACE may not be used for identification purposes in accordance with this Code. See Code C Note for guidance 17D.*

ANNEX A VIDEO IDENTIFICATION

(a) General

1. The arrangements for obtaining and ensuring the availability of a suitable set of images to be used in a video identification must be the responsibility of an identification officer (see *paragraph 3.11* of this Code) who has no direct involvement with the case.

2. The set of images must include the suspect and at least eight other people who, so far as possible, and subject to *paragraph 7*, resemble the suspect in age, general appearance and position in life. Only one suspect shall appear in any set unless there are two suspects of roughly similar appearance, in which case they may be shown together with at least twelve other people.

2A If the suspect has an unusual physical feature, e.g., a facial scar, tattoo or distinctive hairstyle or hair colour which does not appear on the images of the other people that are available to be used, steps may be taken to:

(a) conceal the location of the feature on the images of the suspect and the other people; or

(b) replicate that feature on the images of the other people.

For these purposes, the feature may be concealed or replicated electronically or by any other method which it is practicable to use to ensure that the images of the suspect and other people resemble each other. The identification officer has discretion to choose whether to conceal or replicate the feature and the method to be used.

2B If the identification officer decides that a feature should be concealed or replicated, the reason for the decision and whether the feature was concealed or replicated in the images shown to any eye-witness shall be recorded.

2C If the eye-witness requests to view any image where an unusual physical feature has been concealed or replicated without the feature being concealed or replicated, the identification officer has discretion to allow the eye-witness to view such image(s) if they are available.

3. The images used to conduct a video identification shall, as far as possible, show the suspect and other people in the same positions or carrying out the same sequence of movements. They shall also show the suspect and other people under identical conditions unless the identification officer reasonably believes:

(a) because of the suspect's failure or refusal to co-operate or other reasons, it is not practicable for the conditions to be identical; and

(b) any difference in the conditions would not direct an eye-witness' attention to any individual image.

4. The reasons identical conditions are not practicable shall be recorded on forms provided for the purpose.

5. Provision must be made for each person shown to be identified by number.

6. If police officers are shown, any numerals or other identifying badges must be concealed. If a prison inmate is shown, either as a suspect or not, then either all, or none of, the people shown should be in prison clothing.

7. The suspect or their solicitor, friend, or appropriate adult must be given a reasonable opportunity to see the complete set of images before it is shown to any eye-witness. If the suspect has a reasonable objection to the set of images or any of the participants, the suspect shall be asked to state the reasons for the objection. Steps shall, if practicable, be taken to remove the grounds for objection. If this is not practicable, the suspect and/or their representative shall be told why their objections cannot be met and the objection, the reason given for it and why it cannot be met shall be recorded on forms provided for the purpose. The requirement in *paragraph 2* that the images of the other people 'resemble' the suspect does not require the images to be identical or extremely similar (see *Note A1)*.

8. Before the images are shown in accordance with *paragraph 7,* the suspect or their solicitor shall be provided with details of the first description of the suspect by any eye-witnesses who are to attend the video identification. When a broadcast or publication is made, as in *paragraph 3.38(a)*, the suspect or their solicitor must also be allowed to view any material released to the media by the police for the purpose of recognising or tracing the suspect, provided it is practicable and would not unreasonably delay the investigation.

9. No unauthorised people may be present when the video identification is conducted. The suspect's solicitor, if practicable, shall be given reasonable notification of the time and place the video identification is to be conducted. The suspect's solicitor may only be present at the video identification on request and with the prior agreement of the identification officer, if the officer is satisfied that the solicitor's presence will not deter or distract any eye-witness from viewing the images and making an identification. If the identification officer is not satisfied and does not agree to the request, the reason must be recorded. The solicitor must be informed of the decision and the reason for it. and that they may then make representations about why they should be allowed to be present. The representations may be made orally or in writing, in person or remotely by electronic communication and must be recorded. These representations must be considered by an officer of at least the rank of inspector who is not involved with the investigation and responsibility for this may not be delegated under *paragraph 3.11*. If, after considering the representations, the officer is satisfied that the solicitor's presence will deter or distract the eye-witness, the officer shall inform the solicitor of the decision and reason for it and ensure that any response by the solicitor is also recorded. If allowed to be present, the solicitor is not entitled to communicate in any way with an eye-witness during the procedure but this does not prevent the solicitor from communicating with the identification officer. The suspect may not be present when the images are shown to any eye-witness and is not entitled to be informed of the time and place the video identification procedure is to be conducted. The video identification procedure itself shall be recorded on video with sound. The recording must show all persons present within the sight or hearing of the eye-witness whilst the images are being viewed and must include what the eye-witness says and what is said to them by the identification officer and by any other person present at the video identification procedure. A supervised viewing of the recording of the video identification procedure by the suspect and/or their solicitor may be arranged on request, at the discretion of the investigating officer. Where the recording of the video identification procedure is to be shown to the suspect and/or their solicitor, the investigating officer may arrange for anything in the recording that might allow the eye-witness to be identified to be concealed if the investigating officer considers that this is justified (see *Note A2)*. In accordance with *paragraph 2.18*, the investigating officer may also arrange for anything in that recording that might allow any police officers or police staff to be identified to be concealed.

(b) Conducting the video identification

10. The identification officer is responsible for making the appropriate arrangements to make sure, before they see the set of images, eye-witnesses are not able to communicate with each other about the case, see any of the images which are to be shown, see, or be reminded of, any photograph or description of the suspect or be given any other indication as to the suspect's identity, or overhear an eye-witness who has already seen the material. There must be no discussion with the eye-witness about the composition of the set of images and they must not be told whether a previous eye-witness has made any identification.

11. Only one eye-witness may see the set of images at a time. Immediately before the images are shown, the eye-witness shall be told that the person they saw on a specified earlier occasion may, or may not, appear in the images they are shown and that if they cannot make an identification, they should say so. The eye-witness shall be advised that at any point, they may ask to see a particular part of the set of images or to have a particular image frozen for them to study. Furthermore, it should be pointed out to the eye-witness that there is no limit on how many times they can view the whole set of images or any part

of them. However, they should be asked not to make any decision as to whether the person they saw is on the set of images until they have seen the whole set at least twice.

12. Once the eye-witness has seen the whole set of images at least twice and has indicated that they do not want to view the images, or any part of them, again, the eye-witness shall be asked to say whether the individual they saw in person on a specified earlier occasion has been shown and, if so, to identify them by number of the image. The eye-witness will then be shown that image to confirm the identification, see *paragraph 17*.

13. Care must be taken not to direct the eye-witness' attention to any one individual image or give any indication of the suspect's identity. Where an eye-witness has previously made an identification by photographs, or a computerised or artist's composite or similar likeness, they must not be reminded of such a photograph or composite likeness once a suspect is available for identification by other means in accordance with this Code. Nor must the eye-witness be reminded of any description of the suspect.

13A. If after the video identification procedure has ended, the eye-witness informs any police officer or police staff involved in the post-viewing arrangements that they wish to change their decision about their identification, or they have not made an identification when in fact they could have made one, an accurate record of the words used by the eye-witness and of the circumstances immediately after the procedure ended, shall be made. If the eye-witness has not had an opportunity to communicate with other people about the procedure, the identification officer has the discretion to allow the eye-witness a second opportunity to make an identification by repeating the video identification procedure using the same images but in different positions.

14. After the procedure, action required in accordance with paragraph 3.40 applies.

(c) Image security and destruction

15. Arrangements shall be made for all relevant material containing sets of images used for specific identification procedures to be kept securely and their movements accounted for. In particular, no-one involved in the investigation shall be permitted to view the material prior to it being shown to any witness.

16. As appropriate, *paragraph 3.30* or *3.31* applies to the destruction or retention of relevant sets of images.

(d) Documentation

17. A record must be made of all those participating in, or seeing, the set of images whose names are known to the police.

18. A record of the conduct of the video identification must be made on forms provided for the purpose. This shall include anything said by the witness about any identifications or the conduct of the procedure and any reasons it was not practicable to comply with any of the provisions of this Code governing the conduct of video identifications. This record is in addition to any statement that is taken from any eye-witness after the procedure.

Note for guidance

A1 *The purpose of the video identification is to test the eye-witness' ability to distinguish the suspect from others and it would not be a fair test if all the images shown were identical or extremely similar to each other. The identification officer is responsible for ensuring that the images shown are suitable for the purpose of this test.*

A2 *The purpose of allowing the identity of the eye-witness to be concealed is to protect them in cases when there is information that suspects or their associates, may threaten the witness or cause them harm or when the investigating officer considers that special measures may be required to protect their identity during the criminal process.*

ANNEX B IDENTIFICATION PARADES

(a) General

1. A suspect must be given a reasonable opportunity to have a solicitor or friend present, and the suspect shall be asked to indicate on a second copy of the notice whether or not they wish to do so.

2. An identification parade may take place either in a normal room or one equipped with a screen permitting witnesses to see members of the identification parade without being seen. The procedures for the composition and conduct of the identification parade are the same in both cases, subject to *paragraph 8* (except that an identification parade involving a screen may take place only when the suspect's solicitor, friend or appropriate adult is present or the identification parade is recorded on video).

3. Before the identification parade takes place, the suspect or their solicitor shall be provided with details of the first description of the suspect by any witnesses who are attending the identification parade. When a broadcast or publication is made as in *paragraph 3.38(a)*, the suspect or their solicitor should also be allowed to view any material released to the media by the police for the purpose of identifying and tracing the suspect, provided it is practicable to do so and would not unreasonably delay the investigation.

(b) Identification parades involving prison inmates

4. If a prison inmate is required for identification, and there are no security problems about the person leaving the establishment, they may be asked to participate in an identification parade or video identification.

5. An identification parade may be held in a Prison Department establishment but shall be conducted, as far as practicable under normal identification parade rules. Members of the public shall make up the identification parade unless there are serious security, or control, objections to their admission to the establishment. In such cases, or if a group or video identification is arranged within the establishment, other inmates may participate. If an inmate is the suspect, they are not required to wear prison clothing for the identification parade unless the other people taking part are other inmates in similar clothing, or are members of the public who are prepared to wear prison clothing for the occasion.

(c) Conduct of the identification parade

6. Immediately before the identification parade, the suspect must be reminded of the procedures governing its conduct and cautioned in the terms of Code C, paragraphs 10.5 or 10.6, as appropriate.

7. All unauthorised people must be excluded from the place where the identification parade is held.

8. Once the identification parade has been formed, everything afterwards, in respect of it, shall take place in the presence and hearing of the suspect and any interpreter, solicitor, friend or appropriate adult who is present (unless the identification parade involves a screen, in which case everything said to, or by, any witness at the place where the identification parade is held, must be said in the hearing and presence of the suspect's solicitor, friend or appropriate adult or be recorded on video).

9. The identification parade shall consist of at least eight people (in addition to the suspect) who, so far as possible, resemble the suspect in age, height, general appearance and position in life. Only one suspect shall be included in an identification parade unless there are two suspects of roughly similar appearance, in which case they may be paraded together with at least twelve other people. In no circumstances shall more than two suspects be included in one identification parade and where there are separate identification parades, they shall be made up of different people.

10. If the suspect has an unusual physical feature, e.g., a facial scar, tattoo or distinctive hairstyle or hair colour which cannot be replicated on other members of the identification parade, steps may be taken to conceal the location of that feature on the suspect and the other members of the identification parade if the suspect and their solicitor, or appropriate adult, agree. For example, by use of a plaster or a hat, so that all members of the identification parade resemble each other in general appearance.

11. When all members of a similar group are possible suspects, separate identification parades shall be held for each unless there are two suspects of similar appearance when they may appear on the same identification parade with at least twelve other members of the group who are not suspects. When police officers in uniform form an identification parade any numerals or other identifying badges shall be concealed.

12. When the suspect is brought to the place where the identification parade is to be held, they shall be asked if they have any objection to the arrangements for the identification parade or to any of the other participants in it and to state the reasons for the objection. The suspect may obtain advice from their solicitor or friend, if present, before the identification parade proceeds. If the suspect has a reasonable objection to the arrangements or any of the participants, steps shall, if practicable, be taken to remove the grounds for objection. When it is not practicable to do so, the suspect shall be told why their objections cannot be met and the objection, the reason given for it and why it cannot be met, shall be recorded on forms provided for the purpose.

13. The suspect may select their own position in the line, but may not otherwise interfere with the order of the people forming the line. When there is more than one witness, the suspect must be told, after each witness has left the room, that they can, if they wish, change position in the line. Each position in the line must be clearly numbered, whether by means of a number laid on the floor in front of each identification parade member or by other means.

14. Appropriate arrangements must be made to make sure, before witnesses attend the identification parade, they are not able to:

(i) communicate with each other about the case or overhear a witness who has already seen the identification parade;

(ii) see any member of the identification parade;

(iii) see, or be reminded of, any photograph or description of the suspect or be given any other indication as to the suspect's identity; or

(iv) see the suspect before or after the identification parade.

15. The person conducting a witness to an identification parade must not discuss with them the composition of the identification parade and, in particular, must not disclose whether a previous witness has made any identification.

16. Witnesses shall be brought in one at a time. Immediately before the witness inspects the identification parade, they shall be told the person they saw on a specified earlier occasion may, or may not, be present and if they cannot make an identification, they should say so. The witness must also be told they should not make any decision about whether the person they saw is on the identification parade until they have looked at each member at least twice.

17. When the officer or police staff (see *paragraph 3.11*) conducting the identification procedure is satisfied the witness has properly looked at each member of the identification parade, they shall ask the witness whether the person they saw on a specified earlier occasion is on the identification parade and, if so, to indicate the number of the person concerned, see *paragraph 28*.

18. If the witness wishes to hear any identification parade member speak, adopt any specified posture or move, they shall first be asked whether they can identify any person(s) on the identification parade on the basis of appearance only. When the request is to hear

members of the identification parade speak, the witness shall be reminded that the participants in the identification parade have been chosen on the basis of physical appearance only. Members of the identification parade may then be asked to comply with the witness' request to hear them speak, see them move or adopt any specified posture.

19. If the witness requests that the person they have indicated remove anything used for the purposes of *paragraph 10* to conceal the location of an unusual physical feature, that person may be asked to remove it.

20. If the witness makes an identification after the identification parade has ended, the suspect and, if present, their solicitor, interpreter or friend shall be informed. When this occurs, consideration should be given to allowing the witness a second opportunity to identify the suspect.

21 After the procedure, action required in accordance with *paragraph 3.40* applies.

22. When the last witness has left, the suspect shall be asked whether they wish to make any comments on the conduct of the identification parade.

(d) Documentation

23. A video recording must normally be taken of the identification parade. If that is impracticable, a colour photograph must be taken. A copy of the video recording or photograph shall be supplied, on request, to the suspect or their solicitor within a reasonable time.

24. As appropriate, *paragraph 3.30* or *3.31*, should apply to any photograph or video taken as in *paragraph 23*.

25. If any person is asked to leave an identification parade because they are interfering with its conduct, the circumstances shall be recorded.

26. A record must be made of all those present at an identification parade whose names are known to the police.

27. If prison inmates make up an identification parade, the circumstances must be recorded.

28. A record of the conduct of any identification parade must be made on forms provided for the purpose. This shall include anything said by the witness or the suspect about any identifications or the conduct of the procedure, and any reasons it was not practicable to comply with any of this Code's provisions.

ANNEX C GROUP IDENTIFICATION

(a) General

1. The purpose of this Annex is to make sure, as far as possible, group identifications follow the principles and procedures for identification parades so the conditions are fair to the suspect in the way they test the witness' ability to make an identification.

2. Group identifications may take place either with the suspect's consent and co-operation or covertly without their consent.

3. The location of the group identification is a matter for the identification officer, although the officer may take into account any representations made by the suspect, appropriate adult, their solicitor or friend.

4. The place where the group identification is held should be one where other people are either passing by or waiting around informally, in groups such that the suspect is able to join them and be capable of being seen by the witness at the same time as others in the group. For example people leaving an escalator, pedestrians walking through a shopping centre, passengers on railway and bus stations, waiting in queues or groups or where people are standing or sitting in groups in other public places.

5. If the group identification is to be held covertly, the choice of locations will be limited by the places where the suspect can be found and the number of other people present at that time. In these cases, suitable locations might be along regular routes travelled by the suspect, including buses or trains or public places frequented by the suspect.

6. Although the number, age, sex, race and general description and style of clothing of other people present at the location cannot be controlled by the identification officer, in selecting the location the officer must consider the general appearance and numbers of people likely to be present. In particular, the officer must reasonably expect that over the period the witness observes the group, they will be able to see, from time to time, a number of others whose appearance is broadly similar to that of the suspect.

7. A group identification need not be held if the identification officer believes, because of the unusual appearance of the suspect, none of the locations it would be practicable to use, satisfy the requirements of *paragraph 6* necessary to make the identification fair.

8. Immediately after a group identification procedure has taken place (with or without the suspect's consent), a colour photograph or video should be taken of the general scene, if practicable, to give a general impression of the scene and the number of people present. Alternatively, if it is practicable, the group identification may be video recorded.

9. If it is not practicable to take the photograph or video in accordance with *paragraph 8,* a photograph or film of the scene should be taken later at a time determined by the identification officer if the officer considers it practicable to do so.

10. An identification carried out in accordance with this Code remains a group identification even though, at the time of being seen by the witness, the suspect was on their own rather than in a group.

11. Before the group identification takes place, the suspect or their solicitor shall be provided with details of the first description of the suspect by any witnesses who are to attend the identification. When a broadcast or publication is made, as in *paragraph 3.38(a),* the suspect or their solicitor should also be allowed to view any material released by the police to the media for the purposes of identifying and tracing the suspect, provided that it is practicable and would not unreasonably delay the investigation.

12. After the procedure, action required in accordance with *paragraph 3.40* applies.

(b) Identification with the consent of the suspect

13. A suspect must be given a reasonable opportunity to have a solicitor or friend present. They shall be asked to indicate on a second copy of the notice whether or not they wish to do so.

14. The witness, the person carrying out the procedure and the suspect's solicitor, appropriate adult, friend or any interpreter for the witness, may be concealed from the sight of the individuals in the group they are observing, if the person carrying out the procedure considers this assists the conduct of the identification.

15. The person conducting a witness to a group identification must not discuss with them the forthcoming group identification and, in particular, must not disclose whether a previous witness has made any identification.

16. Anything said to, or by, the witness during the procedure about the identification should be said in the presence and hearing of those present at the procedure.

17. Appropriate arrangements must be made to make sure, before witnesses attend the group identification, they are not able to:

    (i) communicate with each other about the case or overhear a witness who has already been given an opportunity to see the suspect in the group;

    (ii) see the suspect; or

    (iii) see, or be reminded of, any photographs or description of the suspect or be given any other indication of the suspect's identity.

18. Witnesses shall be brought one at a time to the place where they are to observe the group. Immediately before the witness is asked to look at the group, the person conducting the procedure shall tell them that the person they saw on a specified earlier occasion may, or may not, be in the group and that if they cannot make an identification, they should say so. The witness shall be asked to observe the group in which the suspect is to appear. The way in which the witness should do this will depend on whether the group is moving or stationary.

Moving group

19. When the group in which the suspect is to appear is moving, e.g. leaving an escalator, the provisions of *paragraphs 20* to *24* should be followed.

20. If two or more suspects consent to a group identification, each should be the subject of separate identification procedures. These may be conducted consecutively on the same occasion.

21. The person conducting the procedure shall tell the witness to observe the group and ask them to point out any person they think they saw on the specified earlier occasion.

22. Once the witness has been informed as in *paragraph 21* the suspect should be allowed to take whatever position in the group they wish.

23. When the witness points out a person as in *paragraph 21* they shall, if practicable, be asked to take a closer look at the person to confirm the identification. If this is not practicable, or they cannot confirm the identification, they shall be asked how sure they are that the person they have indicated is the relevant person.

24. The witness should continue to observe the group for the period which the person conducting the procedure reasonably believes is necessary in the circumstances for them to be able to make comparisons between the suspect and other individuals of broadly similar appearance to the suspect as in *paragraph 6*.

Stationary groups

25. When the group in which the suspect is to appear is stationary, e.g. people waiting in a queue, the provisions of *paragraphs 26* to *29* should be followed.

26. If two or more suspects consent to a group identification, each should be subject to separate identification procedures unless they are of broadly similar appearance when they may appear in the same group. When separate group identifications are held, the groups must be made up of different people.

27. The suspect may take whatever position in the group they wish. If there is more than one witness, the suspect must be told, out of the sight and hearing of any witness, that they can, if they wish, change their position in the group.

28. The witness shall be asked to pass along, or amongst, the group and to look at each person in the group at least twice, taking as much care and time as possible according to the circumstances, before making an identification. Once the witness has done this, they shall be asked whether the person they saw on the specified earlier occasion is in the group and to indicate any such person by whatever means the person conducting the procedure considers appropriate in the circumstances. If this is not practicable, the witness shall be asked to point out any person they think they saw on the earlier occasion.

29. When the witness makes an indication as in *paragraph 28,* arrangements shall be made, if practicable, for the witness to take a closer look at the person to confirm the identification. If this is not practicable, or the witness is unable to confirm the identification, they shall be asked how sure they are that the person they have indicated is the relevant person.

All cases

30. If the suspect unreasonably delays joining the group, or having joined the group, deliberately conceals themselves from the sight of the witness, this may be treated as a refusal to co-operate in a group identification.

31. If the witness identifies a person other than the suspect, that person should be informed what has happened and asked if they are prepared to give their name and address. There is no obligation upon any member of the public to give these details. There shall be no duty to record any details of any other member of the public present in the group or at the place where the procedure is conducted.

32. When the group identification has been completed, the suspect shall be asked whether they wish to make any comments on the conduct of the procedure.

33. If the suspect has not been previously informed, they shall be told of any identifications made by the witnesses.

(c) Group Identification without the suspect's consent

34. Group identifications held covertly without the suspect's consent should, as far as practicable, follow the rules for conduct of group identification by consent.

35. A suspect has no right to have a solicitor, appropriate adult or friend present as the identification will take place without the knowledge of the suspect.

36. Any number of suspects may be identified at the same time.

(d) Identifications in police stations

37. Group identifications should only take place in police stations for reasons of safety, security or because it is not practicable to hold them elsewhere.

38. The group identification may take place either in a room equipped with a screen permitting witnesses to see members of the group without being seen, or anywhere else in the police station that the identification officer considers appropriate.

39. Any of the additional safeguards applicable to identification parades should be followed if the identification officer considers it is practicable to do so in the circumstances.

(e) Identifications involving prison inmates

40. A group identification involving a prison inmate may only be arranged in the prison or at a police station.

41. When a group identification takes place involving a prison inmate, whether in a prison or in a police station, the arrangements should follow those in *paragraphs 37* to *39*. If a group identification takes place within a prison, other inmates may participate. If an inmate is the suspect, they do not have to wear prison clothing for the group identification unless the other participants are wearing the same clothing.

(f) Documentation

42. When a photograph or video is taken as in *paragraph 8* or *9*, a copy of the photograph or video shall be supplied on request to the suspect or their solicitor within a reasonable time.

43. *Paragraph 3.30* or *3.31*, as appropriate, shall apply when the photograph or film taken in accordance with *paragraph 8* or *9* includes the suspect.

44. A record of the conduct of any group identification must be made on forms provided for the purpose. This shall include anything said by the witness or suspect about any identifications or the conduct of the procedure and any reasons why it was not practicable to comply with any of the provisions of this Code governing the conduct of group identifications.

ANNEX D CONFRONTATION BY AN EYE-WITNESS

1. Before the confrontation takes place, the eye-witness must be told that the person they saw on a specified earlier occasion may, or may not, be the person they are to confront and that if they are not that person, then the witness should say so.

2. Before the confrontation takes place the suspect or their solicitor shall be provided with details of the first description of the suspect given by any eye-witness who is to attend. When a broadcast or publication is made, as in *paragraph 3.38(a)*, the suspect or their solicitor should also be allowed to view any material released to the media for the purposes of recognising or tracing the suspect, provided it is practicable to do so and would not unreasonably delay the investigation.

3. Force may not be used to make the suspect's face visible to the eye-witness.

4. Confrontation must take place in the presence of the suspect's solicitor, interpreter or friend unless this would cause unreasonable delay.

5. The suspect shall be confronted independently by each eye-witness, who shall be asked "Is this the person?". If the eye-witness identifies the person but is unable to confirm the identification, they shall be asked how sure they are that the person is the one they saw on the earlier occasion.

6. The confrontation should normally take place in the police station, either in a normal room or one equipped with a screen permitting the eye-witness to see the suspect without being seen. In both cases, the procedures are the same except that a room equipped with a screen may be used only when the suspect's solicitor, friend or appropriate adult is present or the confrontation is recorded on video.

7. After the procedure, action required in accordance with *paragraph 3.40* applies.

ANNEX E SHOWING PHOTOGRAPHS TO EYE-WITNESSES

(a) Action

1. An officer of sergeant rank or above shall be responsible for supervising and directing the showing of photographs. The actual showing may be done by another officer or police staff, see *paragraph 3.11*.

2. The supervising officer must confirm the first description of the suspect given by the eye-witness has been recorded before they are shown the photographs. If the supervising officer is unable to confirm the description has been recorded they shall postpone showing the photographs.

3. Only one eye-witness shall be shown photographs at any one time. Each witness shall be given as much privacy as practicable and shall not be allowed to communicate with any other eye-witness in the case.

4. The eye-witness shall be shown not less than twelve photographs at a time, which shall, as far as possible, all be of a similar type.

5. When the eye-witness is shown the photographs, they shall be told the photograph of the person they saw on a specified earlier occasion may, or may not, be amongst them and if they cannot make an identification, they should say so. The eye-witness shall also be told they should not make a decision until they have viewed at least twelve photographs. The eye-witness shall not be prompted or guided in any way but shall be left to make any selection without help.

6. If an eye-witness makes an identification from photographs, unless the person identified is otherwise eliminated from enquiries or is not available, other eye-witnesses shall not be shown photographs. But both they, and the eye-witness who has made the identification, shall be asked to attend a video identification, an identification parade or group identification unless there is no dispute about the suspect's identification.

7. If the eye-witness makes a selection but is unable to confirm the identification, the person showing the photographs shall ask them how sure they are that the photograph they have indicated is the person they saw on the specified earlier occasion.

8. When the use of a computerised or artist's composite or similar likeness has led to there being a known suspect who can be asked to participate in a video identification, appear on an identification parade or participate in a group identification, that likeness shall not be shown to other potential eye-witnesses.

9. When an eye-witness attending a video identification, an identification parade or group identification has previously been shown photographs or computerised or artist's composite or similar likeness (and it is the responsibility of the officer in charge of the investigation to make the identification officer aware that this is the case), the suspect and their solicitor must be informed of this fact before the identification procedure takes place.

10. None of the photographs shown shall be destroyed, whether or not an identification is made, since they may be required for production in court. The photographs shall be numbered and a separate photograph taken of the frame or part of the album from which the eye-witness made an identification as an aid to reconstituting it.

(b) Documentation

11. Whether or not an identification is made, a record shall be kept of the showing of photographs on forms provided for the purpose. This shall include anything said by the eye-witness about any identification or the conduct of the procedure, any reasons it was not practicable to comply with any of the provisions of this Code governing the showing of photographs and the name and rank of the supervising officer.

12. The supervising officer shall inspect and sign the record as soon as practicable.

ANNEX F FINGERPRINTS, SAMPLES AND FOOTWEAR IMPRESSIONS — DESTRUCTION AND SPECULATIVE SEARCHES

Part A: Fingerprints and samples

Paragraphs 1 to 12 summarise and update information which is available at:

https://www.gov.uk/government/publications/protection-of-freedoms-act-2012-dna-and-fingerprint-provisions/protection-of-freedoms-act-2012-how-dna-and-fingerprint-evidence-is-protected-in-law

DNA samples

1. A DNA sample is an individual's biological material, containing all of their genetic information. The Act requires all DNA samples to be destroyed within 6 months of being taken. This allows sufficient time for the sample to be analysed and a DNA profile to be produced for use on the database.

2. The only exception to this is if the sample is or may be required for disclosure as evidence, in which case it may be retained for as long as this need exists under the Criminal Procedure and Investigations Act 1996.

DNA profiles and fingerprints

3. A DNA profile consists of a string of 16 pairs of numbers and 2 letters (XX for women, XY for men) to indicate gender. This number string is stored on the National DNA Database (NDNAD). It allows the person to be identified if they leave their DNA at a crime scene.

4. Fingerprints are usually scanned electronically from the individual in custody and the images stored on IDENT1, the national fingerprint database.

Retention Periods: Fingerprints and DNA profiles

5. The retention period depends on the outcome of the investigation of the recordable offence in connection with which the fingerprints and DNA samples was taken, the age of the person at the time the offence was committed and whether the *recordable* offence is a qualifying offence and whether it is an excluded offence (See Table *Notes (a)* to *(c))* , as follows:

Table – Retention periods

(a) Convictions

Age when offence committed	Outcome	Retention Period
Any age	Convicted or given a caution or youth caution for a recordable offence which is also a qualifying offence	INDEFINITE
18 or over	Convicted or given a caution for a recordable offence which is NOT a qualifying offence	INDEFINITE
Under 18	Convicted or given a youth caution for a recordable offence which is NOT a qualifying offence.	1st conviction or youth caution – 5 years plus length of any prison sentence. Indefinite if prison sentence 5 years or more 2nd conviction or youth caution: Indefinite

(b) Non-Convictions

Age when offence committed	Outcome	Retention Period
Any age	Charged but not convicted of a recordable qualifying offence.	3 years plus a 2 year extension if granted by a District Judge (or indefinite if the individual has a previous conviction for a recordable offence which is not excluded)
Any age	Arrested for, but not charged with, a recordable qualifying offence	3 years if granted by the Biometrics Commissioner plus a 2 year extension if granted by a District Judge (or indefinite if the individual has a previous conviction for a recordable offence which is not excluded)
Any age	Arrested for or charged with a recordable offence which is not a qualifying offence.	Indefinite if the person has a previous conviction for a recordable offence which is not excluded otherwise NO RETENTION)
18 or over	Given Penalty Notice for Disorder for recordable offence	2 years

Table Notes:

(a) A 'recordable' offence is one for which the police are required to keep a record. Generally speaking, these are imprisonable offences; however, it also includes a number of non-imprisonable offences such as begging and taxi touting. The police are not able to take or retain the DNA or fingerprints of an individual who is arrested for an offence which is not recordable.

(b) A 'qualifying' offence is one listed under section 65A of the Police and Criminal Evidence Act 1984 (the list comprises sexual, violent, terrorism and burglary offences).

(c) An 'excluded' offence is a recordable offence which is not a qualifying offence, was committed when the individual was under 18, for which they received a sentence of fewer than 5 years imprisonment and is the only recordable offence for which the person has been convicted

Speculative searches

6. Where the retention framework above requires the deletion of a person's DNA profile and fingerprints, the Act first allows a *speculative search* of their DNA and fingerprints against DNA and fingerprints obtained from crime scenes which are stored on NDNAD and IDENT1. Once the speculative search has been completed, the profile and fingerprints are deleted unless there is a match, in which case they will be retained for the duration of any investigation and thereafter in accordance with the retention framework (e.g. if that investigation led to a conviction for a qualifying offence, they would be retained indefinitely).

Extensions of retention period

7. For qualifying offences, PACE allows chief constables to apply for extensions to the given retention periods for DNA profiles and fingerprints if considered necessary for prevention or detection of crime.

8. Section 20 of the Protection of Freedoms Act 2012 established the independent office of Commissioner for the Retention and Use of Biometric Material ('the 'Biometrics Commissioner'). For details, see https://www.gov.uk/government/organisations/biometrics-commissioner.

9. Where an individual is arrested for, but not charged with, a qualifying offence, their DNA profile and fingerprint record will normally be deleted. However, the police can apply to the Biometrics Commissioner for permission to retain their DNA profile and fingerprint record for a period of 3 years. The application must be made within 28 days of the decision not to proceed with a prosecution.

10. If the police make such an application, the Biometrics Commissioner would first give both them and the arrested individual an opportunity to make written representations and then, taking into account factors including the age and vulnerability of the victim(s) of the alleged offences, and their relationship to the suspect, make a decision on whether or not retention is appropriate.

11. If after considering the application, the Biometrics Commissioner decides that retention is not appropriate, the DNA profile and fingerprint record in question must be destroyed.

12. If the Biometrics Commissioner agrees to allow retention, the police will be able to retain that individual's DNA profile and fingerprint record for a period of 3 years from the date the samples were taken. At the end of that period, the police will be able to apply to a District Judge (Magistrates' Courts) for a single 2 year extension to the retention period. If the application is rejected, the force must then destroy the DNA profile and fingerprint record.

Part B: Footwear impressions

13. Footwear impressions taken in accordance with section 61A of PACE (see *paragraphs 4.16* to *4.21*) may be retained for as long as is necessary for purposes related to the prevention or detection of crime, the investigation of an offence or the conduct of a prosecution.

Part C: Fingerprints, samples and footwear impressions taken in connection with a criminal investigation from a person *not suspected of committing* the offence under investigation for elimination purposes.

14. When fingerprints, footwear impressions or DNA samples are taken from a person in connection with an investigation and the person is *not suspected of having committed the offence*, see *Note F1*, they must be destroyed as soon as they have fulfilled the purpose for which they were taken unless:

    (a) they were taken for the purposes of an investigation of an offence for which a person has been convicted; and

    (b) fingerprints, footwear impressions or samples were also taken from the convicted person for the purposes of that investigation.

    However, subject to *paragraph 14,* the fingerprints, footwear impressions and samples, and the information derived from samples, may not be used in the investigation of any offence or in evidence against the person who is, or would be, entitled to the destruction of the fingerprints, footwear impressions and samples, see *Note F2.*

15. The requirement to destroy fingerprints, footwear impressions and DNA samples, and information derived from samples and restrictions on their retention and use in *paragraph 14* do not apply if the person gives their written consent for their fingerprints, footwear impressions or sample to be retained and used after they have fulfilled the purpose for which they were taken, see *Note F1.* This consent can be withdrawn at any time.

16. When a person's fingerprints, footwear impressions or sample are to be destroyed:

    (a) any copies of the fingerprints and footwear impressions must also be destroyed; and

    (b) neither the fingerprints, footwear impressions, the sample, or any information derived from the sample, may be used in the investigation of any offence or in evidence against the person who is, or would be, entitled to its destruction.

Notes for guidance

F1 Fingerprints, footwear impressions and samples given voluntarily for the purposes of elimination play an important part in many police investigations. It is, therefore, important to make sure innocent volunteers are not deterred from participating and their consent to their fingerprints, footwear impressions and DNA being used for the purposes of a specific investigation is fully informed and voluntary. If the police or volunteer seek to have the fingerprints, footwear impressions or samples retained for use after the specific investigation ends, it is important the volunteer's consent to this is also fully informed and voluntary. The volunteer must be told that they may withdraw their consent at any time.

The consent must be obtained in writing using current nationally agreed forms provided for police use according to the purpose for which the consent is given. This purpose may be either:

- *DNA/fingerprints/footwear impressions - to be used only for the purposes of a specific investigation; or*
- *DNA/fingerprints/footwear impressions - to be used in the specific investigation* ***and*** *retained by the police for future use.*

To minimise the risk of confusion:

- *if a police officer or member of police staff has any doubt about:*
  - *how the consent forms should be completed and signed, or*
  - *whether a consent form they propose to use and refer to is fully compliant with the current nationally agreed form,*

  the relevant national police helpdesk (for DNA or fingerprints) should be contacted.
- *in each case, the meaning of consent should be explained orally and care taken to ensure the oral explanation accurately reflects the contents of the written form the person is to be asked to sign.*

F2 The provisions for the retention of fingerprints, footwear impressions and samples in paragraph 15 allow for all fingerprints, footwear impressions and samples in a case to be available for any subsequent miscarriage of justice investigation.

ANNEX G REQUIREMENT FOR A PERSON TO ATTEND A POLICE STATION FOR FINGERPRINTS AND SAMPLES (*PARAGRAPHS 4.4,* *6.2A* AND *6.6A*).

1. A requirement under Schedule 2A for a person to attend a police station to have fingerprints or samples taken:
   (a) must give the person a period of at least seven days within which to attend the police station; and
   (b) may direct them to attend at a specified time of day or between specified times of day.
2. When specifying the period and times of attendance, the officer making the requirements must consider whether the fingerprints or samples could reasonably be taken at a time when the person is required to attend the police station for any other reason. See *Note G1*.
3. An officer of the rank of inspector or above may authorise a period shorter than 7 days if there is an urgent need for person's fingerprints or sample for the purposes of the investigation of an offence. The fact of the authorisation and the reasons for giving it must be recorded as soon as practicable.
4. The constable making a requirement and the person to whom it applies may agree to vary it so as to specify any period within which, or date or time at which, the person is to attend. However, variation shall not have effect for the purposes of enforcement, unless it is confirmed by the constable in writing.

Notes for guidance

G1 The specified period within which the person is to attend need not fall within the period allowed (if applicable) for making the requirement.

G2 To justify the arrest without warrant of a person who fails to comply with a requirement, (see paragraphs 4.4(b) and 6.7(b) above), the officer making the requirement, or confirming a variation, should be prepared to explain how, when and where the requirement was made or the variation was confirmed and what steps were taken to ensure the person understood what to do and the consequences of not complying with the requirement.

YOUR NOTES

YOUR NOTES

YOUR NOTES

YOUR NOTES

YOUR NOTES

Adapted and published by GRANGIS under the OGL Licence.
GRANGIS - UK PUBLISHING 2022.
Thank you for taking the time to leave us a review regarding this edition"

★★★★★

For further inquiries, please feel free to contact us at:
www.grangis.com / contact@grangis.com

www.ingramcontent.com/pod-product-compliance
Lightning Source LLC
LaVergne TN
LVHW022321200926
848481LV00004B/1389